Conference of the North American Chapter of the Association for Computational Linguistics: Human Language Technologies (NAACL HLT 2021)

Tutorials

Online
6 – 11 June 2021

ISBN: 978-1-7138-3013-9

Printed from e-media with permission by:

Curran Associates, Inc.
57 Morehouse Lane
Red Hook, NY 12571

CURRAN ASSOCIATES INC. proceedings.com

Some format issues inherent in the e-media version may also appear in this print version.

Printed with permission by Curran Associates, Inc. (2021)

Association for Computational Linguistics
209 N. Eighth Street
Stroudsburg, Pennsylvania 18360

Phone: 1-570-476-8006
Fax: 1-570-476-0860

acl@aclweb.org

Additional copies of this publication are available from:

Curran Associates, Inc.
57 Morehouse Lane
Red Hook, NY 12571 USA
Phone: 845-758-0400
Fax: 845-758-2633
Email: curran@proceedings.com
Web: www.proceedings.com

NAACL-HLT 2021

The 2021 Conference of the North American Chapter of the Association for Computational Linguistics: Human Language Technologies

Tutorials

June 6, 2021

Introduction

Welcome to the Tutorials Session of NAACL HLT 2021.

The NAACL 2021 tutorials session is organized to give conference attendees a comprehensive introduction from expert researchers to a topic of importance drawn from our research field. This year, the tutorials committee consisted of tutorials chairs from four conferences: EACL, NAACL, ACL-IJCNLP and EMNLP. A total of 35 tutorial submissions were received, of which 6 were selected for presentation at NAACL 2021. The tutorials selected this year are on topics ranging from transformers to crowdsourcing. We would like to thank Kristina Toutanova (NAACL general chair), and Steven Bethard (NAACL publications chair) for their help during the process. We hope you enjoy the tutorials.

NAACL 2021 Tutorial Co-chairs
Greg Kondrak, University of Alberta
Kalina Bontcheva, University of Sheffield
Dan Gillick, Google Research

Tutorial Chairs

Greg Kondrak, University of Alberta
Kalina Bontcheva, University of Sheffield
Dan Gillick, Google Research

Table of Contents

Pretrained Transformers for Text Ranking: BERT and Beyond
Andrew Yates, Rodrigo Nogueira and Jimmy Lin 1

Fine-grained Interpretation and Causation Analysis in Deep NLP Models
Hassan Sajjad, Narine Kokhlikyan, Fahim Dalvi and Nadir Durrani 5

Deep Learning on Graphs for Natural Language Processing
Lingfei Wu, Yu Chen, Heng Ji and Yunyao Li 11

A Tutorial on Evaluation Metrics used in Natural Language Generation
Mitesh M. Khapra and Ananya B. Sai 15

Beyond Paragraphs: NLP for Long Sequences
Iz Beltagy, Arman Cohan, Hannaneh Hajishirzi, Sewon Min and Matthew Peters 20

Crowdsourcing Natural Language Data at Scale: A Hands-On Tutorial
Alexey Drutsa, Dmitry Ustalov, Valentina Fedorova, Olga Megorskaya and Daria Baidakova . . . 25

Conference Program

6 Jun 2021 (all times PDT, UTC-7)

08:00–12:00 *Pretrained Transformers for Text Ranking: BERT and Beyond*
Andrew Yates, Rodrigo Nogueira and Jimmy Lin

08:00–12:00 *Fine-grained Interpretation and Causation Analysis in Deep NLP Models*
Hassan Sajjad, Narine Kokhlikyan, Fahim Dalvi and Nadir Durrani

08:00–12:00 *Deep Learning on Graphs for Natural Language Processing*
Lingfei Wu, Yu Chen, Heng Ji and Yunyao Li

08:00–12:00 *A Tutorial on Evaluation Metrics used in Natural Language Generation*
Mitesh M. Khapra and Ananya B. Sai

08:00–12:00 *Beyond Paragraphs: NLP for Long Sequences*
Iz Beltagy, Arman Cohan, Hannaneh Hajishirzi, Sewon Min and Matthew Peters

16:00–20:00 *Crowdsourcing Natural Language Data at Scale: A Hands-On Tutorial*
Alexey Drutsa, Dmitry Ustalov, Valentina Fedorova, Olga Megorskaya and Daria Baidakova

Pretrained Transformers for Text Ranking: BERT and Beyond

Andrew Yates,[1] **Rodrigo Nogueira,**[2] and **Jimmy Lin**[2]
[1] Max Planck Institute for Informatics
[2] David R. Cheriton School of Computer Science, University of Waterloo

1 Overview

The goal of text ranking is to generate an ordered list of texts retrieved from a corpus in response to a query for a particular task. Although the most common formulation of text ranking is search, instances of the task can also be found in many text processing applications. This tutorial provides an overview of text ranking with neural network architectures known as transformers, of which BERT (Bidirectional Encoder Representations from Transformers) (Devlin et al., 2019) is the best-known example. These models produce high quality results across many domains, tasks, and settings.

This tutorial, which is based on the preprint (Lin et al., 2020a) of a forthcoming book to be published by Morgan and & Claypool under the Synthesis Lectures on Human Language Technologies series, provides an overview of existing work as a single point of entry for practitioners who wish to deploy transformers for text ranking in real-world applications and researchers who wish to pursue work in this area. We cover a wide range of techniques, grouped into two categories: transformer models that perform reranking in multi-stage ranking architectures and learned dense representations that perform ranking directly.

2 Multi-Stage Ranking Architectures

The most straightforward application of transformers to text ranking is to convert the task into a text classification problem, and then sort the texts to be ranked based on the probability that each item belongs to the relevant class. The first application of BERT to text ranking, by Nogueira and Cho (2019), used BERT in exactly this manner. This *relevance classification* approach is usually deployed in a module that reranks candidate texts from an initial keyword search engine.

One key limitation of BERT is its inability to handle long input sequences and hence difficulty in ranking texts beyond a certain length (e.g., "full-length" documents such as news articles). This limitation is addressed by a number of models (Nogueira and Cho, 2019; Akkalyoncu Yilmaz et al., 2019; Dai and Callan, 2019b; MacAvaney et al., 2019; Wu et al., 2020; Li et al., 2020), and a simple retrieve-then-rerank approach can be elaborated into a multi-stage architecture with reranker pipelines (Nogueira et al., 2019a; Matsubara et al., 2020; Soldaini and Moschitti, 2020) that balance effectiveness and efficiency. On top of multi-stage ranking architectures, researchers have proposed additional innovations, including query expansion (Zheng et al., 2020), document expansion (Nogueira et al., 2019b; Nogueira and Lin, 2019) and term importance prediction (Dai and Callan, 2019a, 2020).

A natural question that arises is, "What's beyond BERT?" We describe efforts to build ranking models that are faster (i.e., lower inference latency), that are better (i.e., higher ranking effectiveness), or that manifest interesting tradeoffs between effectiveness and efficiency. These include ranking models that leverage BERT variants (Li et al., 2020), exploit knowledge distillation to train more compact student models (Gao et al., 2020a), and other transformer architectures, including ground-up redesign efforts (Hofstätter et al., 2020b; Mitra et al., 2020) and adapting pretrained sequence-to-sequence models (Nogueira et al., 2020; dos Santos et al., 2020). These discussions set up a natural transition to ranking based on dense representations, the other main category of approaches we cover.

3 Learned Dense Representations

Arguably, the single biggest benefit brought about by modern deep learning techniques to text ranking is the move away from sparse signals, mostly

Proceedings of NAACL-HLT 2021: Tutorials, pages 1–4

limited to exact matches, to dense representations that are able to capture semantic matches to better model relevance. The potential of continuous dense representations for natural language analysis was first demonstrated nearly a decade ago with word embeddings on word analogy tasks (Mikolov et al., 2013). As soon as researchers tried to build representations for any larger spans of text: phrases, sentences, paragraphs, and documents, the same issues that arise in text ranking come into focus. In fact, ranking with dense representations predates BERT by many years (Huang et al., 2013; De Boom et al., 1999; Mitra et al., 2016; Henderson et al., 2017; Wu et al., 2018; Zamani et al., 2018).

In the context of transformers, the general setup of ranking with dense representations involves learning transformer-based encoders that convert queries and texts into dense, fixed-size vectors. In the simplest approach, ranking becomes the problem of approximate nearest neighbor (ANN) search based on some simple metric such as cosine similarity (Lee et al., 2019; Xiong et al., 2020; Lu et al., 2020; Reimers and Gurevych, 2019; MacAvaney et al., 2020; Gao et al., 2020b; Karpukhin et al., 2020; Zhan et al., 2020; Qu et al., 2020; Hofstätter et al., 2020a; Lin et al., 2020b). However, recognizing that accurate ranking cannot be captured via simple metrics, researchers have explored using more complex machinery to compare dense representations (Humeau et al., 2020; Khattab and Zaharia, 2020). Here, as with multi-stage ranking architectures, limitations on text length and effectiveness–efficiency tradeoffs are important considerations. It becomes increasingly difficult to accurately capture the semantics of longer texts with fixed-sized representations, and increasingly complex comparison architectures increase latency and may necessitate reranking designs.

4 Looking Ahead

Learned dense representations complement sparse (bag-of-words) term-based representations central to keyword search techniques that have dominated the landscape for more than half a century. Together, hybrid multi-stage approaches (e.g., combining both ranking and reranking) present a promising future direction.

Despite the excitement in directly ranking with dense learned representations, we anticipate that reranking transformers will remain important in the future. For one, results from dense retrieval can usually be reranked to achieve even higher effectiveness. At a high level, there are three current approaches: *apply* existing transformer models with minimal modifications, *adapt* existing transformer models, perhaps adding additional architectural elements, and *redesign* transformer-based architectures from scratch. Which approach will prove to be most effective? The jury's still out.

Related, in NLP we see that the GPT family (Brown et al., 2020) continues to push the frontier of larger models, more compute, and more data. For text ranking, is the simple answer to build bigger models? Probably not, since ranking has important differences with many traditional NLP tasks. But if not, what are the evolving roles of zero-shot learning, distant supervision, transfer learning, domain adaptation, data augmentation, and task-specific fine-tuning? This remains an interesting open research question.

While there are aspects of text ranking with pretrained transformers that are well understood, many promising directions await further exploration. Looking ahead, we anticipate many more exciting developments!

5 Presenter Bios

Andrew Yates is a Senior Researcher at the Max Planck Institute for Informatics, where he heads a research group working in areas of information retrieval and natural language processing. Yates received his Ph.D. in Computer Science from Georgetown University in 2016.

Rodrigo Nogueira is a post-doctoral researcher at the University of Waterloo, an adjunct professor at UNICAMP, Brazil, and a senior research scientist at NeuralMind, Brazil. Nogueira received his Ph.D. from New York University in 2019.

Jimmy Lin holds the David R. Cheriton Chair in the David R. Cheriton School of Computer Science at the University of Waterloo. Prior to 2015, he was a faculty at the University of Maryland, College Park. Lin received his Ph.D. in Electrical Engineering and Computer Science from the Massachusetts Institute of Technology in 2004.

Acknowledgments

This work was supported in part by the Canada First Research Excellence Fund and the Natural Sciences and Engineering Research Council (NSERC) of Canada.

References

Zeynep Akkalyoncu Yilmaz, Wei Yang, Haotian Zhang, and Jimmy Lin. 2019. Cross-domain modeling of sentence-level evidence for document retrieval. In *Proceedings of the 2019 Conference on Empirical Methods in Natural Language Processing and the 9th International Joint Conference on Natural Language Processing (EMNLP-IJCNLP)*, pages 3490–3496, Hong Kong, China.

Tom B. Brown, Benjamin Mann, Nick Ryder, Melanie Subbiah, Jared Kaplan, Prafulla Dhariwal, Arvind Neelakantan, Pranav Shyam, Girish Sastry, Amanda Askell, Sandhini Agarwal, Ariel Herbert-Voss, Gretchen Krueger, Tom Henighan, Rewon Child, Aditya Ramesh, Daniel M. Ziegler, Jeffrey Wu, Clemens Winter, Christopher Hesse, Mark Chen, Eric Sigler, Mateusz Litwin, Scott Gray, Benjamin Chess, Jack Clark, Christopher Berner, Sam McCandlish, Alec Radford, Ilya Sutskever, and Dario Amodei. 2020. Language models are few-shot learners. *arXiv:2005.14165*.

Zhuyun Dai and Jamie Callan. 2019a. Context-aware sentence/passage term importance estimation for first stage retrieval. *arXiv:1910.10687*.

Zhuyun Dai and Jamie Callan. 2019b. Deeper text understanding for IR with contextual neural language modeling. In *Proceedings of the 42nd International ACM SIGIR Conference on Research and Development in Information Retrieval (SIGIR 2019)*, pages 985–988, Paris, France.

Zhuyun Dai and Jamie Callan. 2020. Context-aware document term weighting for ad-hoc search. In *Proceedings of The Web Conference 2020*, WWW '20, page 1897–1907.

Cedric De Boom, Steven Van Canneyt, Thomas Demeester, and Bart Dhoedt. 1999. Representation learning for very short texts using weighted word embedding aggregation. *Pattern Recognition Letters*, 80(C):150–156.

Jacob Devlin, Ming-Wei Chang, Kenton Lee, and Kristina Toutanova. 2019. BERT: Pre-training of deep bidirectional transformers for language understanding. In *Proceedings of the 2019 Conference of the North American Chapter of the Association for Computational Linguistics: Human Language Technologies, Volume 1 (Long and Short Papers)*, pages 4171–4186, Minneapolis, Minnesota.

Luyu Gao, Zhuyun Dai, and Jamie Callan. 2020a. Understanding bert rankers under distillation. In *Proceedings of the 2020 ACM SIGIR International Conference on Theory of Information Retrieval (ICTIR 2020)*, pages 149–152.

Luyu Gao, Zhuyun Dai, Zhen Fan, and Jamie Callan. 2020b. Complementing lexical retrieval with semantic residual embedding. *arXiv:2004.13969*.

Matthew Henderson, Rami Al-Rfou, Brian Strope, Yun hsuan Sung, Laszlo Lukacs, Ruiqi Guo, Sanjiv Kumar, Balint Miklos, and Ray Kurzweil. 2017. Efficient natural language response suggestion for Smart Reply. *arXiv:1705.00652*.

Sebastian Hofstätter, Sophia Althammer, Michael Schröder, Mete Sertkan, and Allan Hanbury. 2020a. Improving efficient neural ranking models with cross-architecture knowledge distillation. *arXiv:2010.02666*.

Sebastian Hofstätter, Markus Zlabinger, and Allan Hanbury. 2020b. Interpretable & time-budget-constrained contextualization for re-ranking. In *Proceedings of the 24th European Conference on Artificial Intelligence (ECAI 2020)*, Santiago de Compostela, Spain.

Po-Sen Huang, Xiaodong He, Jianfeng Gao, Li Deng, Alex Acero, and Larry Heck. 2013. Learning deep structured semantic models for web search using clickthrough data. In *Proceedings of 22nd International Conference on Information and Knowledge Management (CIKM 2013)*, pages 2333–2338, San Francisco, California.

Samuel Humeau, Kurt Shuster, Marie-Anne Lachaux, and Jason Weston. 2020. Poly-encoders: Architectures and pre-training strategies for fast and accurate multi-sentence scoring. In *Proceedings of the 8th International Conference on Learning Representations (ICLR 2020)*.

Vladimir Karpukhin, Barlas Oguz, Sewon Min, Patrick Lewis, Ledell Wu, Sergey Edunov, Danqi Chen, and Wen-tau Yih. 2020. Dense passage retrieval for open-domain question answering. In *Proceedings of the 2020 Conference on Empirical Methods in Natural Language Processing (EMNLP)*, pages 6769–6781.

Omar Khattab and Matei Zaharia. 2020. ColBERT: Efficient and effective passage search via contextualized late interaction over BERT. In *Proceedings of the 43rd International ACM SIGIR Conference on Research and Development in Information Retrieval (SIGIR 2020)*, pages 39–48.

Kenton Lee, Ming-Wei Chang, and Kristina Toutanova. 2019. Latent retrieval for weakly supervised open domain question answering. In *Proceedings of the 57th Annual Meeting of the Association for Computational Linguistics*, pages 6086–6096, Florence, Italy.

Canjia Li, Andrew Yates, Sean MacAvaney, Ben He, and Yingfei Sun. 2020. PARADE: Passage representation aggregation for document reranking. *arXiv:2008.09093*.

Jimmy Lin, Rodrigo Nogueira, and Andrew Yates. 2020a. Pretrained transformers for text ranking: BERT and beyond. *arXiv:2010.06467*.

Sheng-Chieh Lin, Jheng-Hong Yang, and Jimmy Lin. 2020b. Distilling dense representations for ranking using tightly-coupled teachers. *arXiv:2010.11386*.

Wenhao Lu, Jian Jiao, and Ruofei Zhang. 2020. TwinBERT: Distilling knowledge to twin-structured bert models for efficient retrieval. *arXiv:2002.06275*.

Sean MacAvaney, Franco Maria Nardini, Raffaele Perego, Nicola Tonellotto, Nazli Goharian, and Ophir Frieder. 2020. Expansion via prediction of importance with contextualization. In *Proceedings of the 43rd International ACM SIGIR Conference on Research and Development in Information Retrieval (SIGIR 2020)*, page 1573–1576.

Sean MacAvaney, Andrew Yates, Arman Cohan, and Nazli Goharian. 2019. CEDR: Contextualized embeddings for document ranking. In *Proceedings of the 42nd International ACM SIGIR Conference on Research and Development in Information Retrieval (SIGIR 2019)*, pages 1101–1104, Paris, France.

Yoshitomo Matsubara, Thuy Vu, and Alessandro Moschitti. 2020. Reranking for efficient transformer-based answer selection. In *Proceedings of the 43rd International ACM SIGIR Conference on Research and Development in Information Retrieval (SIGIR 2020)*, page 1577–1580.

Tomas Mikolov, Ilya Sutskever, Kai Chen, Greg S. Corrado, and Jeff Dean. 2013. Distributed representations of words and phrases and their compositionality. In *Advances in Neural Information Processing Systems 26 (NIPS 2013)*, pages 3111–3119, Lake Tahoe, California.

Bhaskar Mitra, Sebastian Hofstatter, Hamed Zamani, and Nick Craswell. 2020. Conformer-kernel with query term independence for document retrieval. *arXiv:2007.10434*.

Bhaskar Mitra, Eric Nalisnick, Nick Craswell, and Rich Caruana. 2016. A dual embedding space model for document ranking. *arXiv:1602.01137v1*.

Rodrigo Nogueira and Kyunghyun Cho. 2019. Passage re-ranking with BERT. *arXiv:1901.04085*.

Rodrigo Nogueira, Zhiying Jiang, Ronak Pradeep, and Jimmy Lin. 2020. Document ranking with a pre-trained sequence-to-sequence model. In *Findings of the Association for Computational Linguistics: EMNLP 2020*, pages 708–718.

Rodrigo Nogueira and Jimmy Lin. 2019. From doc2query to docTTTTTquery.

Rodrigo Nogueira, Wei Yang, Kyunghyun Cho, and Jimmy Lin. 2019a. Multi-stage document ranking with BERT. In *arXiv:1910.14424*.

Rodrigo Nogueira, Wei Yang, Jimmy Lin, and Kyunghyun Cho. 2019b. Document expansion by query prediction. In *arXiv:1904.08375*.

Yingqi Qu, Yuchen Ding, Jing Liu, Kai Liu, Ruiyang Ren, Xin Zhao, Daxiang Dong, Hua Wu, and Haifeng Wang. 2020. RocketQA: An optimized training approach to dense passage retrieval for open-domain question answering. *arXiv:2010.08191*.

Nils Reimers and Iryna Gurevych. 2019. Sentence-BERT: Sentence embeddings using Siamese BERT-networks. In *Proceedings of the 2019 Conference on Empirical Methods in Natural Language Processing and the 9th International Joint Conference on Natural Language Processing (EMNLP-IJCNLP)*, pages 3982–3992, Hong Kong, China.

Cicero Nogueira dos Santos, Xiaofei Ma, Ramesh Nallapati, Zhiheng Huang, and Bing Xiang. 2020. Beyond [CLS] through ranking by generation. In *Proceedings of the 2020 Conference on Empirical Methods in Natural Language Processing (EMNLP)*, pages 1722–1727.

Luca Soldaini and Alessandro Moschitti. 2020. The cascade transformer: an application for efficient answer sentence selection. In *Proceedings of the 58th Annual Meeting of the Association for Computational Linguistics*, pages 5697–5708.

Ledell Wu, Adam Fisch, Sumit Chopra, Keith Adams, Antoine Bordes, and Jason Weston. 2018. StarSpace: Embed all the things! In *Proceedings of the Thirty-Second AAAI Conference on Artificial Intelligence (AAAI 2018)*.

Zhijing Wu, Jiaxin Mao, Yiqun Liu, Jingtao Zhan, Yukun Zheng, Min Zhang, and Shaoping Ma. 2020. Leveraging passage-level cumulative gain for document ranking. In *Proceedings of The Web Conference 2020*, WWW '20, page 2421–2431.

Lee Xiong, Chenyan Xiong, Ye Li, Kwok-Fung Tang, Jialin Liu, Paul Bennett, Junaid Ahmed, and Arnold Overwijk. 2020. Approximate nearest neighbor negative contrastive learning for dense text retrieval. *arXiv:2007.00808*.

Hamed Zamani, Mostafa Dehghani, W. Bruce Croft, Erik Learned-Miller, and Jaap Kamps. 2018. From neural re-ranking to neural ranking: Learning a sparse representation for inverted indexing. In *Proceedings of the 27th ACM International Conference on Information and Knowledge Management (CIKM 2018)*, pages 497–506, Torino, Italy.

Jingtao Zhan, Jiaxin Mao, Yiqun Liu, Min Zhang, and Shaoping Ma. 2020. RepBERT: Contextualized text embeddings for first-stage retrieval. *arXiv:2006.15498*.

Zhi Zheng, Kai Hui, Ben He, Xianpei Han, Le Sun, and Andrew Yates. 2020. BERT-QE: Contextualized Query Expansion for Document Re-ranking. In *Findings of the Association for Computational Linguistics: EMNLP 2020*, pages 4718–4728.

Fine-grained Interpretation and Causation Analysis in Deep NLP Models

Hassan Sajjad Narine Kokhlikyan* Fahim Dalvi Nadir Durrani

{hsajjad,faimaduddin,ndurrani}@hbku.edu.qa
Qatar Computing Research Institute, HBKU Research Complex, Doha 5825, Qatar
narine@fb.com
*Facebook AI, 1 Facebook Way, Menlo Park, CA 94025, USA

1 Introduction

Deep neural networks have constantly pushed the state-of-the-art performance in natural language processing and are considered as the de facto modeling approach in solving most complex NLP tasks such as machine translation, summarization and question-answering. Despite the benefits and the usefulness of deep neural networks at-large, their opaqueness is a major cause of concern. Interpreting neural networks is considered important for increasing trust in AI systems, providing additional information to decision makers, and assisting ethical decision making (Lipton, 2016).

Interpretation of neural network models is a broad area of research. Significant work has analyzed network at representation-level (Belinkov et al., 2017; Conneau et al., 2018; Adi et al., 2016; Tenney et al., 2019), and at neuron-level (Bau et al., 2020; Mu and Andreas, 2020a; Bau et al., 2019; Dalvi et al., 2019a). Others have experimented with various behavioural studies to analyze models (Gulordava et al., 2018; Linzen et al., 2016; Marvin and Linzen, 2018). Moreover, a number of studies cover the importance of input features and neurons with respect to a prediction (Dhamdhere et al., 2018a; Lundberg and Lee, 2017; Tran et al., 2018). The topic of interpretation of neural models has gained a lot of attention in a last couple of years. For example, it has been added as a regular track in major *CL conferences. There is an annual workshop, BlackboxNLP, dedicated for this purpose. The ACL 2020 and EMNLP 2020[1] featured tutorials on the topic (Belinkov et al., 2020). The ACL tutorial focused on two subareas of interpretation which are the representation analysis and the behavioral studies. The EMNLP tutorial is solely focused on behavioral studies i.e. assess a model's behavior using constructed examples. Both of these tutorials serves as a great starting point for the new researchers in this area.

The representation analysis, also called as structural analysis, is useful to understand how various core linguistic properties are learned in the model. However, the analysis suffers from a few limitations. It mainly focuses at interpreting full vector representations and does not study the role of fine-grained components in the representation i.e. neurons. Also the findings of representation analysis do not link with the cause of a prediction (Belinkov and Glass, 2019). While the behavioral analysis evaluates model predictions, it does not typically connect them with the influence of the input features and the internal components of a model (Vig et al., 2020).

In this tutorial, we aim to present and discuss the research work on interpreting fine-grained components of a model from two perspectives, i) fine-grained interpretation, ii) causation analysis. The former will introduce methods to analyze individual neurons and a group of neurons with respect to a desired language property or a task. The latter will bring up the role of neurons and input features in explaining decisions made by the model. We will cover important research questions such as i) how is knowledge distributed across the model components? ii) what knowledge learned within the model is used for specific predictions? iii) does the inhibition of specific knowledge in the model change predictions? iv) how do different modeling and optimization choices impact the underlying knowledge?

Recent work on interpreting neurons has shown that in-addition to gaining better understanding of the inner workings of neural networks, the neuron-level interpretation has applications in model distillation (Rethmeier et al., 2020), domain adaptation (Gu et al., 2021) or efficient feature selection (Dalvi et al., 2020) e.g., by removing unimportant neurons, facilitating architecture search, and mitigating model bias by identifying neurons responsible for

[1] https://2020.emnlp.org/tutorials

Proceedings of NAACL-HLT 2021: Tutorials, pages 5–10
June 6–11, 2021.

sensitive attributes like gender, race or politeness (Bau et al., 2019; Vig et al., 2020). These recent works are not only enabling better understanding of these networks, but are also leading towards better, fairer and more environmental-friendly models, which are all important goals for the Artificial Intelligence community at large.

2 Description

The tutorial is divided into two main parts: i) fine-grained interpretation, and ii) causation analysis. The first part of the tutorial covers methods that align neurons to human interpretable concepts or study the most salient neurons in the network. We cluster these methods into four groups i) Visualization Methods (Karpathy et al., 2015; Li et al., 2016a), ii) Corpus Selection (Kádár et al., 2017; Poerner et al., 2018; Na et al., 2019; Mu and Andreas, 2020b), iii) Neuron Probing (Dalvi et al., 2019a; Lakretz et al., 2019; Valipour et al., 2019; Durrani et al., 2020) and iv) Unsupervised Methods (Bau et al., 2019; Torroba Hennigen et al., 2020; Wu et al., 2020; Michael et al., 2020). We will discuss evaluation methods that are used to measure the effectiveness of an interpretation method, such as accuracy, control tasks (Hewitt and Liang, 2019) and ablation studies (Li et al., 2016b; Lillian et al., 2018; Dalvi et al., 2019a; Lakretz et al., 2019). Moreover, we will cover various applications of these methods that go beyond interpretation such as efficient transfer learning (Dalvi et al., 2020), controlling system's behavior (Bau et al., 2019; Suau et al., 2020), generating explanations (Mu and Andreas, 2020b) and domain adaptation (Gu et al., 2021).

The second part, *Causation Analysis*, will focus on methods that seek to characterize the role of neurons and layers towards a specific prediction. More concretely, we will discuss gradient and perturbation-based attribution algorithms such as Integrated Gradients (Sundararajan et al., 2017), Layer Conductance (Dhamdhere et al., 2018b), Saliency (Simonyan et al., 2014), SHapley Additive exPlanations(SHAP) (Lundberg and Lee, 2017) and showcase how they can help us to identify important neurons in different layers of a deep neural network. Besides that we will also dive deep into more recent and advanced attribution algorithms that take feature or neuron interactions into account. More specifically, we will look into Integrated Hessians (Janizek et al., 2020), Shapely Taylor index (Dhamdhere et al., 2020) and Archipelago (Tsang et al., 2020).

Lastly, we will mention various open source toolkits and libraries that provide implementation of notable techniques in the area. A few examples of the toolkits are: Captum (Kokhlikyan et al., 2020), InterpretML[2], NeuroX (Dalvi et al., 2019b), Ecco[3] and Diagnnose (Jumelet and Hupkes, 2019). We will walk-through how some of these tools can be used for fine-grained interpretation and causation analysis.

Throughout the tutorial, our goal will also be to critically evaluate where the strengths and weakness of each of the presented methods lie, and provide ideas and recommendations around future directions.

3 Outline

1. **Introduction:** We will introduce the topic and motivate it by providing the vision of model interpretability, and how it leads towards fair and ethical models that generalize well. We will then describe various forms of interpretation and will outline the scope of the tutorial (15 minutes).

2. **Fine-grained Interpretation:** We will present and discuss the work on neuron-level interpretation. (90 minutes)
   - Methods (30 minutes)
   - Evaluation (15 minutes)
   - Findings (30 minutes)
   - Practical (15 minutes)

3. **Causation Analysis:** In causation analysis we will present various methods on interpreting model predictions with respect to input features and individual neurons. (60 minutes)
   - Methods (30 minutes)
   - Evaluation (10 minutes)
   - Practical (20 minutes)

4. **Concept-based Interpretation of Prediction:** This part will aim to bridge the gap between fine-grained interpretation and causation analysis. We will discuss how fine-grained interpretation and causation analysis can be combined to establish concept-based

[2] https://interpret.ml/
[3] https://www.eccox.io/

interpretation of model predictions. (10 minutes)

5. **Discussion:** The last part will discuss the overall challenges that the current work faces and suggest future directions. (10 minutes)

4 Prerequisites

We assume basic knowledge of the deep learning and familiarity with the LSTM-based and transformer-based pre-trained models such as ELMo (Peters et al., 2018) and BERT (Devlin et al., 2019). Additionally, some familiarity with natural language processing tasks such as, named entity tagging, natural language inference, etc. would be useful but not mandatory. We do not expect participants to have familiarity with the research on the interpretation and analysis of deep models. Familiarity with Python, Pytorch and Transformers library (Wolf et al., 2019) would be useful to understand the practical part.

5 Reading List

- In order to get an overview of the interpretation field, trainees may look at the following survey papers: Belinkov and Glass (2019) and Danilevsky et al. (2020).
- Fine-grained analysis and its Applications: Bau et al. (2019); Dalvi et al. (2019a); Mu and Andreas (2020b); Suau et al. (2020) etc.
- Causation analysis: Lundberg and Lee (2017) provides an overview of various methods introduced in literature. For more details, see the following papers: Voita et al. (2020); Sundararajan et al. (2017); Dhamdhere et al. (2018b); Ribeiro et al. (2016); Janizek et al. (2020)

In addition to the above list, interested trainees may look at the papers mentioned in Section 2.

6 Instructor Information (Alphabetic order

Fahim Dalvi, Software Engineer, Qatar Computing Research Institute, Qatar
Email: faimaduddin@hbku.edu.qa
Website: `https://fdalvi.github.io`

Fahim Dalvi is an experienced Software Engineer with a demonstrated history of working in the research industry and is currently employed at the Qatar Computing Research Institute. Fahim's research is centered around the intersection of Natural Language Processing and Deep Learning, and he has worked on wide variety of problems in these fields including Machine Translation, Language Modelling and Explainability in Deep Neural Networks. He also spends his time converting research into practical applications, with a focus on scalable web applications. Fahim also spends some time every year mentoring and teaching Deep Learning at Fall and Summer schools.

Hassan Sajjad, Senior Research Scientist, Qatar Computing Research Institute, Qatar

Email: hsajjad@hbku.edu.qa
Website: `https://hsajjad.github.io`

Hassan Sajjad is a Senior Research Scientist at the Qatar Computing Research Institute (QCRI), HBKU. His research interests include the interpretation of deep neural models, machine translation, domain adaptation, and natural language processing involving low-resource and morphologically-rich languages. His research work has been published in several prestigious venues such as CL, CSL, ICLR, ACL, NAACL and EMNLP. His work in collaboration with MIT and Harvard on the interpretation of deep models has also been featured in several tech blogs including MIT News. Hassan co-organized BlackboxNLP 2020, and the WMT 2019/2020 machine translation robustness task. He served as an area chair for the analysis and interpretability, NLP Application, and machine translation tracks at various *CL conferences. In addition, Hassan has been regularly teaching courses on deep learning internationally at various spring and summer schools.

Narine Kokhlikyan, Research Scientist, Facebook AI

Email: narine@fb.com
Website: `https://www.linkedin.com/in/narine-k-88916721/`

Narine is a Research Scientist focusing on Model Interpretability as part of PyTorch team at Facebook. Her research interests include the understanding of Deep Neural Network internals and their predictions across different applications such as Natural Language Processing, Computer Vision and Recommender Systems. In the recent years she gave talks and presented tutorials on Model Interpretability at KDD 2020 and NeurIPS 2019. Before joining Facebook Narine worked on Natural Language Processing, Time Series Analysis and numerical optimizations.

Nadir Durrani, Research Scientist, Qatar Computing Research Institute, Qatar
Email: ndurrani@hbku.edu.qa
Website: `http://alt.qcri.org/~ndurrani/`

Nadir Durrani is a Research Scientist at the Arabic Language Technologies group at Qatar Computing Research Institute. His research interests include interpretation of neural networks, neural and statistical machine translation (with focus on reordering, domain adaptation, transliteration, dialectal translation, pivoting, closely related and morphologically rich languages), eye-tracking for MT evaluation, spoken language translation and speech synthesis. His recent work focuses on analyzing contextualized representations with the focus of linguistic interpretation, manipulation, feature selection and model distillation. His work on analyzing deep neural networks has been published at venues like Computational Linguistics, *ACL, AAAI and ICLR. Nadir has been involved in co-organizing workshops such as simultaneous machine translation and WMT 2019/2020 Machine translation robustness task. He regularly serves as program committee and has served as Area chair at ACL and AAAI this year.

References

Yossi Adi, Einat Kermany, Yonatan Belinkov, Ofer Lavi, and Yoav Goldberg. 2016. Fine-grained analysis of sentence embeddings using auxiliary prediction tasks. *CoRR*, abs/1608.04207.

Anthony Bau, Yonatan Belinkov, Hassan Sajjad, Nadir Durrani, Fahim Dalvi, and James Glass. 2019. Identifying and controlling important neurons in neural machine translation. In *International Conference on Learning Representations*.

David Bau, Jun-Yan Zhu, Hendrik Strobelt, Agata Lapedriza, Bolei Zhou, and Antonio Torralba. 2020. Understanding the role of individual units in a deep neural network. *Proceedings of the National Academy of Sciences*.

Yonatan Belinkov, Sebastian Gehrmann, and Ellie Pavlick. 2020. Interpretability and analysis in neural NLP. In *Proceedings of the 58th Annual Meeting of the Association for Computational Linguistics: Tutorial Abstracts*, pages 1–5, Online. Association for Computational Linguistics.

Yonatan Belinkov and James Glass. 2019. Analysis methods in neural language processing: A survey. *Transactions of the Association for Computational Linguistics*, 7:49–72.

Yonatan Belinkov, Lluís Màrquez, Hassan Sajjad, Nadir Durrani, Fahim Dalvi, and James Glass. 2017. Evaluating layers of representation in neural machine translation on part-of-speech and semantic tagging tasks. In *Proceedings of the Eighth International Joint Conference on Natural Language Processing (Volume 1: Long Papers)*, pages 1–10, Taipei, Taiwan. Asian Federation of Natural Language Processing.

Alexis Conneau, German Kruszewski, Guillaume Lample, Loïc Barrault, and Marco Baroni. 2018. What you can cram into a single $&!#* vector: Probing sentence embeddings for linguistic properties. In *Proceedings of the 56th Annual Meeting of the Association for Computational Linguistics (Volume 1: Long Papers)*, pages 2126–2136, Melbourne, Australia. Association for Computational Linguistics.

Fahim Dalvi, Nadir Durrani, Hassan Sajjad, Yonatan Belinkov, D. Anthony Bau, and James Glass. 2019a. What is one grain of sand in the desert? analyzing individual neurons in deep nlp models. In *Proceedings of the Thirty-Third AAAI Conference on Artificial Intelligence (AAAI, Oral presentation)*.

Fahim Dalvi, Avery Nortonsmith, D. Anthony Bau, Yonatan Belinkov, Hassan Sajjad, Nadir Durrani, and James Glass. 2019b. Neurox: A toolkit for analyzing individual neurons in neural networks. In *AAAI Conference on Artificial Intelligence (AAAI)*.

Fahim Dalvi, Hassan Sajjad, Nadir Durrani, and Yonatan Belinkov. 2020. Analyzing redundancy in pretrained transformer models. In *Proceedings of the 2020 Conference on Empirical Methods in Natural Language Processing (EMNLP-2020)*, Online. Association for Computational Linguistics.

Marina Danilevsky, Kun Qian, Ranit Aharonov, Yannis Katsis, Ban Kawas, and Prithviraj Sen. 2020. A survey of the state of explainable AI for natural language processing. In *Proceedings of the 1st Conference of the Asia-Pacific Chapter of the Association for Computational Linguistics and the 10th International Joint Conference on Natural Language Processing*, pages 447–459, Suzhou, China. Association for Computational Linguistics.

Jacob Devlin, Ming-Wei Chang, Kenton Lee, and Kristina Toutanova. 2019. BERT: Pre-training of deep bidirectional transformers for language understanding. In *Proceedings of the 2019 Conference of the North American Chapter of the Association for Computational Linguistics: Human Language Technologies, Volume 1 (Long and Short Papers)*, Minneapolis, Minnesota. Association for Computational Linguistics.

Kedar Dhamdhere, Ashish Agarwal, and Mukund Sundararajan. 2020. The shapley taylor interaction index.

Kedar Dhamdhere, Mukund Sundararajan, and Qiqi Yan. 2018a. How important is a neuron? *CoRR*, abs/1805.12233.

Kedar Dhamdhere, Mukund Sundararajan, and Qiqi Yan. 2018b. How important is a neuron?

Nadir Durrani, Hassan Sajjad, Fahim Dalvi, and Yonatan Belinkov. 2020. Analyzing individual neurons in pre-trained language models. In *Proceedings of the 2020 Conference on Empirical Methods in Natural Language Processing (EMNLP)*, pages 4865–4880, Online. Association for Computational Linguistics.

Shuhao Gu, Yang Feng, and Wanying Xie. 2021. Pruning-then-expanding model for domain adaptation of neural machine translation.

Kristina Gulordava, Piotr Bojanowski, Edouard Grave, Tal Linzen, and Marco Baroni. 2018. Colorless green recurrent networks dream hierarchically. In *Proceedings of the 2018 Conference of the North American Chapter of the Association for Computational Linguistics: Human Language Technologies, Volume 1 (Long Papers)*, pages 1195–1205, New Orleans, Louisiana. Association for Computational Linguistics.

John Hewitt and Percy Liang. 2019. Designing and interpreting probes with control tasks. In *Proceedings of the 2019 Conference on Empirical Methods in Natural Language Processing and the 9th International Joint Conference on Natural Language Processing (EMNLP-IJCNLP)*, pages 2733–2743, Hong Kong, China. Association for Computational Linguistics.

Joseph D. Janizek, Pascal Sturmfels, and Su-In Lee. 2020. Explaining explanations: Axiomatic feature interactions for deep networks.

Jaap Jumelet and Dieuwke Hupkes. 2019. diagnnose: A neural net analysis library.

Ákos Kádár, Grzegorz Chrupała, and Afra Alishahi. 2017. Representation of linguistic form and function in recurrent neural networks. *Computational Linguistics*, 43(4):761–780.

Andrej Karpathy, Justin Johnson, and Li Fei-Fei. 2015. Visualizing and understanding recurrent networks.

Narine Kokhlikyan, Vivek Miglani, Miguel Martin, Edward Wang, Bilal Alsallakh, Jonathan Reynolds, Alexander Melnikov, Natalia Kliushkina, Carlos Araya, Siqi Yan, and Orion Reblitz-Richardson. 2020. Captum: A unified and generic model interpretability library for PyTorch.

Yair Lakretz, German Kruszewski, Theo Desbordes, Dieuwke Hupkes, Stanislas Dehaene, and Marco Baroni. 2019. The emergence of number and syntax units in LSTM language models. In *Proceedings of the 2019 Conference of the North American Chapter of the Association for Computational Linguistics: Human Language Technologies, Volume 1 (Long and Short Papers)*, pages 11–20, Minneapolis, Minnesota. Association for Computational Linguistics.

Jiwei Li, Xinlei Chen, Eduard Hovy, and Dan Jurafsky. 2016a. Visualizing and understanding neural models in NLP. In *Proceedings of the 2016 Conference of the North American Chapter of the Association for Computational Linguistics: Human Language Technologies*, pages 681–691, San Diego, California. Association for Computational Linguistics.

Jiwei Li, Will Monroe, and Dan Jurafsky. 2016b. Understanding neural networks through representation erasure. *CoRR*, abs/1612.08220.

Peter Lillian, Richard Meyes, and Tobias Meisen. 2018. Ablation of a robot's brain: Neural networks under a knife. *CoRR*, abs/1812.05687.

Tal Linzen, Emmanuel Dupoux, and Yoav Goldberg. 2016. Assessing the ability of LSTMs to learn syntax-sensitive dependencies. *Transactions of the Association for Computational Linguistics*, 4:521–535.

Zachary C Lipton. 2016. The Mythos of Model Interpretability. In *ICML Workshop on Human Interpretability in Machine Learning (WHI)*.

Scott M Lundberg and Su-In Lee. 2017. A unified approach to interpreting model predictions. In I. Guyon, U. V. Luxburg, S. Bengio, H. Wallach, R. Fergus, S. Vishwanathan, and R. Garnett, editors, *Advances in Neural Information Processing Systems 30*, pages 4765–4774. Curran Associates, Inc.

Rebecca Marvin and Tal Linzen. 2018. Targeted syntactic evaluation of language models. In *Proceedings of the 2018 Conference on Empirical Methods in Natural Language Processing*, pages 1192–1202, Brussels, Belgium. Association for Computational Linguistics.

Julian Michael, Jan A. Botha, and Ian Tenney. 2020. Asking without telling: Exploring latent ontologies in contextual representations. In *Proceedings of the 2020 Conference on Empirical Methods in Natural Language Processing (EMNLP)*, pages 6792–6812, Online. Association for Computational Linguistics.

Jesse Mu and Jacob Andreas. 2020a. Compositional explanations of neurons.

Jesse Mu and Jacob Andreas. 2020b. Compositional explanations of neurons. *CoRR*, abs/2006.14032.

Seil Na, Yo Joong Choe, Dong-Hyun Lee, and Gunhee Kim. 2019. Discovery of natural language concepts in individual units of cnns. *CoRR*, abs/1902.07249.

Matthew Peters, Mark Neumann, Mohit Iyyer, Matt Gardner, Christopher Clark, Kenton Lee, and Luke Zettlemoyer. 2018. Deep contextualized word representations. In *Proceedings of the 2018 Conference of the North American Chapter of the Association for Computational Linguistics: Human Language Technologies, Volume 1 (Long Papers)*, New Orleans, Louisiana. Association for Computational Linguistics.

Nina Poerner, Benjamin Roth, and Hinrich Schütze. 2018. Interpretable textual neuron representations for NLP. In *Proceedings of the 2018 EMNLP Workshop BlackboxNLP: Analyzing and Interpreting Neural Networks for NLP*, pages 325–327, Brussels, Belgium. Association for Computational Linguistics.

Nils Rethmeier, Vageesh Kumar Saxena, and Isabelle Augenstein. 2020. Tx-ray: Quantifying and explaining model-knowledge transfer in (un-)supervised NLP. In *Proceedings of the Thirty-Sixth Conference on Uncertainty in Artificial Intelligence, UAI 2020, virtual online, August 3-6, 2020*, page 197. AUAI Press.

Marco Túlio Ribeiro, Sameer Singh, and Carlos Guestrin. 2016. "why should I trust you?": Explaining the predictions of any classifier. *CoRR*, abs/1602.04938.

Karen Simonyan, Andrea Vedaldi, and Andrew Zisserman. 2014. Deep inside convolutional networks: Visualising image classification models and saliency maps.

Xavier Suau, Luca Zappella, and Nicholas Apostoloff. 2020. Finding experts in transformer models. *CoRR*, abs/2005.07647.

Mukund Sundararajan, Ankur Taly, and Qiqi Yan. 2017. Axiomatic attribution for deep networks.

Ian Tenney, Dipanjan Das, and Ellie Pavlick. 2019. BERT rediscovers the classical NLP pipeline. In *Proceedings of the 57th Annual Meeting of the Association for Computational Linguistics*, pages 4593–4601, Florence, Italy. Association for Computational Linguistics.

Lucas Torroba Hennigen, Adina Williams, and Ryan Cotterell. 2020. Intrinsic probing through dimension selection. In *Proceedings of the 2020 Conference on Empirical Methods in Natural Language Processing (EMNLP)*, pages 197–216, Online. Association for Computational Linguistics.

Ke Tran, Arianna Bisazza, and Christof Monz. 2018. The Importance of Being Recurrent for Modeling Hierarchical Structure. *arXiv preprint arXiv:1803.03585*.

Michael Tsang, Sirisha Rambhatla, and Yan Liu. 2020. How does this interaction affect me? interpretable attribution for feature interactions.

Mehrdad Valipour, En-Shiun Annie Lee, Jaime R. Jamacaro, and Carolina Bessega. 2019. Unsupervised transfer learning via BERT neuron selection. *CoRR*, abs/1912.05308.

Jesse Vig, Sebastian Gehrmann, Yonatan Belinkov, Sharon Qian, Daniel Nevo, Yaron Singer, and Stuart Shieber. 2020. Causal Mediation Analysis for Interpreting Neural NLP: The Case of Gender Bias. *arXiv preprint arXiv:2004.12265*.

Elena Voita, Rico Sennrich, and Ivan Titov. 2020. Analyzing the source and target contributions to predictions in neural machine translation.

Thomas Wolf, Lysandre Debut, Victor Sanh, Julien Chaumond, Clement Delangue, Anthony Moi, Pierric Cistac, Tim Rault, R'emi Louf, Morgan Funtowicz, and Jamie Brew. 2019. Huggingface's transformers: State-of-the-art natural language processing. *ArXiv*, abs/1910.03771.

John Wu, Hassan Belinkov, Yonatan Sajjad, Nadir Durrani, Fahim Dalvi, and James Glass. 2020. Similarity Analysis of Contextual Word Representation Models. In *Proceedings of the 58th Annual Meeting of the Association for Computational Linguistics (ACL)*, Seattle. Association for Computational Linguistics.

Deep Learning on Graphs for Natural Language Processing

Lingfei Wu
JD.COM Silicon Valley Research Center
lwu@email.wm.edu

Yu Chen
Facebook AI
hugochen@fb.com

Heng Ji
University of Illinois Urbana-Champaign
hengji@illinois.edu

Yunyao Li
IBM Research AI
yunyaoli@us.ibm.com

Keywords: Natural Language Processing, Deep Learning, Graph Learning, Graph Neural Networks
Type of the tutorial: cutting-edge
Suggested duration: 3.5 hours
Estimated number of participants: 300
Estimate of what % of the tutorial covers work by the tutorial presenters vs. work by other researchers: 40% vs. 60%.
Open access: We agree to allow the publication of our slides and video recording of our tutorial in the ACL Anthology. Other teaching material (i.e., data and code) will be openly available.

1 Description

Deep learning has become the dominant approach in Natural Language Processing (NLP) research today, especially when applied on large scale corpora. Conventionally, sentences are typically considered as a sequence of tokens in NLP tasks. Hence, popular deep learning techniques such as recurrent neural networks (RNN) and convolutional neural networks (CNN) have been widely applied for modeling text sequence.

However, there is a rich variety of NLP problems that can be best expressed with a graph structure. For instance, the structural and semantic information in sequence data (e.g., various syntactic parsing trees like dependency parsing trees and semantic parsing graphs like abstract meaning representation (AMR) graphs) can be exploited to augment original sequence data by incorporating the task-specific knowledge. As a result, these graph-structured data can encode complicated pairwise relationships between entity tokens for learning more informative representations. However, it is well-known that deep learning techniques that were disruptive for Euclidean data such as images or sequence data such as text are not immediately applicable to graph-structured data. Therefore, this gap has driven a tide in research for deep learning on graphs, especially in development of graph neural networks (GNN).

This wave of research at the intersection of deep learning on graphs and NLP has influenced a variety of NLP tasks. There has seen a surge of interests in applying/developing various types of GNNs and achieved considerable success in many NLP tasks, ranging from classification tasks like sentence classification, semantic role labeling and relation extraction, to generation tasks like machine translation, question generation and summarization. Despite these successes, deep learning on graphs for NLP still face many challenges, namely,

- Automatically transforming original text sequence data into highly graph-structured data. Such challenges are profound in NLP since most of the NLP tasks use the text sequence as the original inputs. Automatic graph construction from the text sequence to take into account underlying structural information is a critical step in the use of graph neural network models for NLP problems.

- Effectively modeling complex data that involves mapping between graph-based inputs and other highly structured output data such as sequences, trees, and graph data with multi-types in both nodes and edges. Many generation tasks in NLP such as SQL-to-Text, Text-to-AMR, Text-to-KB are emblematic of such challenges.

This tutorial of **D**eep **L**earning on **G**raphs for **N**atural **L**anguage **P**rocessing (DLG4NLP) is timely for the computational linguistics community, and covers relevant and interesting topics, including automatic graph construction for NLP, graph representation learning for NLP, various advanced GNN based models (e.g., graph2seq, graph2tree,

Proceedings of NAACL-HLT 2021: Tutorials, pages 11–14
June 6–11, 2021. ©2021 Association for Computational Linguistics

and graph2graph) for NLP, and the applications of GNNs in various NLP tasks (e.g., machine translation, natural language generation, information extraction and semantic parsing). The intended audiences for this tutorial mainly include graduate students and researchers in the field of Natural Language Processing and industry professionals who want to know how the state-of-the-art deep learning on graphs techniques can help solve important yet challenging Natural Language Processing problems.

In addition, hands-on demonstration sessions will be included to help the audience gain practical experience on applying GNNs to solve challenging NLP problems using our recently developed open source library – Graph4NLP, the first library for researchers and practitioners for easy use of graph neural networks for various NLP tasks. After attending the tutorial, the audience are expected to 1) have a comprehensive understanding of basic concepts of deep learning on graphs for NLP; 2) learn major recent advances of research in the intersection of NLP and GNNs; and 3) explore novel research opportunities of GNNs for NLP, and learn how to use or even design novel algorithms with GNNs for effectively coping with various NLP tasks.

We will start with a broad overview of various NLP problems that deal with graph structured data, and highlight some challenges of modeling graph-structured data in the field of NLP with traditional graph-based algorithms (e.g., random walk methods, spectral graph clustering, graph kernels). We will then introduce the general idea as well as some commonly used models of GNNs, which have been an emerging popular tool to deal with graph structured data. After the introduction of NLP tasks on graph data and graph neural networks, we will describe some important yet challenging techniques for deep learning on graphs for NLP, including automatic graph construction from text, graph representation learning for NLP and various advanced GNN based models (e.g., graph2seq, graph2tree, and graph2graph) for NLP. Some representative NLP applications are introduced following the methods. We also include a hands-on demonstration session on how to quickly build GNN-based models for solving NLP tasks using our recently developed open source library Graph4NLP, which was designed for the easy use of GNNs for NLP. We will summarize the tutorial and highlight some open directions in the end of this tutorial. The Introduction, Methodologies, Applications, Hands-on Demonstration, and Conclusion and Open Directions form the five segments of this tutorial.

2 Prerequisites

The audience is expected to have some basic understanding of natural language processing and deep learning. However, the tutorial will be presented at college junior/senior level and should be comfortably followed by academic researchers and industrial practitioners.

3 Tutorial Outline

The intended duration of this tutorial is 3.5 hours, including a half hour break.

I. (20 minutes) Introduction
   1. Natural Language Processing: A Graph Perspective
   2. Graph Based Algorithms for Natural Language Processing
   3. Deep Learning on Graphs: Graph Neural Networks
      i. Foundations
      ii. Methodologies
      iii. Applications in Natural Language Processing: An Overview
      iv. High-level DLG4NLP Roadmap

II. (70 minutes) Methodologies
   1. Automatic Graph Construction from Text
      i. Static Graph Construction
      ii. Dynamic Graph Construction
   2. Graph Representation Learning for NLP
      i. Graph Neural Networks for Improved Text Representation
      ii. Graph Neural Networks for Joint Text & Knowledge Representation
      iii. Graph Neural Networks for Various Graph Types
   3. GNN Based Encoder-Decoder Models
      i. Graph-to-Sequence Models
      ii. Graph-to-Tree Models

III. (60 minutes) Applications
   1. Semantic Parsing
   2. Machine Reading Comprehension

3. Information Extraction
4. Natural Language Generation
5. Machine Translation

IV. (20 minutes) Hands-on Demonstration

1. A Brief Overview of the Graph4NLP Library
2. Live Demo

V. (10 minutes) Conclusion and Open Directions

4 Reading List

We aim to make the tutorial self-contained. For trainees interested in reading important studies before the tutorial, we recommend the following papers regarding GNNs (Kipf and Welling, 2016; Li et al., 2015; Hamilton et al., 2017), automatic graph construction for NLP (Bastings et al., 2017; Chen et al., 2020b,a), joint text and knowledge representation learning (Feng et al., 2020; Lin et al., 2020), modeling directed graphs (Xu et al., 2018; Chen et al., 2020b) and heterogeneous graphs (Bastings et al., 2017; Chen et al., 2020c), and GNN based encoder-decoder models (Xu et al., 2018; Chen et al., 2020b; Li et al., 2020).

5 Diversity

Beside the state-of-the-art deep learning on graphs techniques we are planning to cover, we will discuss how these graph-based Deep Learning techniques can be used in several NLP applications that exploit multilingual data, including but not limited to Machine Translation and Information Extraction. Our tutorial lectures are full of diversities from many perspectives. Our team have male and female researchers(two female tutors and two male tutors); We are from three different institutions including IBM Research, UIUC, and Facebook AI; We are senior, middle-career, and junior-career researchers. We are researchers and professors from academic institutions and industrial labs.

6 Presenters

Lingfei Wu is a Principal Scientist at JD.COM Silicon Valley Research Center. Previously, he was a research staff member and team leader at IBM Research. He has published more than 80 top-ranked conference and journal papers and is a co-inventor of more than 40 filed US patents. Because of the high commercial value of his patents, he has received several invention achievement awards and has been appointed as IBM Master Inventors, class of 2020. He was the recipients of the Best Paper Award and Best Student Paper Award of several conferences such as IEEE ICC'19, AAAI workshop on DLGMA'20 and KDD workshop on DLG'19. His research has been featured in numerous media outlets, including NatureNews, YahooNews, Venturebeat, and TechTalks. He has co-organized 10+ conferences (KDD, AAAI, IEEE BigData) and is the founding co-chair for Workshops of Deep Learning on Graphs (with KDD'21, AAAI'21, AAAI'20, KDD'20, KDD'19, and IEEE BigData'19). He has currently served as Associate Editor for IEEE Transactions on Neural Networks and Learning Systems, ACM Transactions on Knowledge Discovery from Data and International Journal of Intelligent Systems. Lingfei Wu has given many tutorials/keynote presentations in deep learning on graphs for natural language processing in multiple workshops in KDD'20, CVPR'20, AAAI'20, and Machine Learning & Artificial Intelligence'20.
Email: lwu@email.wm.edu
Homepage: `https://sites.google.com/a/email.wm.edu/teddy-lfwu/`.

Yu Chen is a Research Scientist at Facebook AI. He got his PhD degree in Computer Science from Rensselaer Polytechnic Institute. His research interests lie at the intersection of Machine Learning (Deep Learning), and Natural Language Processing, with a particular emphasis on the fast-growing field of Graph Neural Networks and their applications in various domains. His work has been published in top-ranked conferences including but not limited to NeurIPS, ICML, ICLR, AAAI, IJCAI, NAACL, KDD, WSDM, ISWC, and AMIA. He was the recipient of the Best Student Paper Award of AAAI DLGMA'20. He has served as PC members in many conferences (e.g., ACL, EMNLP, NAACL, EACL, AAAI, IJCAI and KDD) and journals (e.g., TNNLS, IJIS, TKDE, TKDD and DAMI).
Email: hugochen@fb.com
Homepage: `http://academic.hugochan.net`

Heng Ji is a professor at the Computer Science Department of University of Illinois at Urbana-Champaign. She has received many awards including "AI's 10 to Watch" Award by IEEE Intelligent Systems in 2013, NSF CAREER award

in 2009, PACLIC2012 Best paper runner-up, "Best of ICDM2013" paper award, and "Best of SDM2013" paper award. She has served as the Program Committee Co-Chair of NAACL-HLT2018, NLP-NABD2018, NLPCC2015, CSCKG2016 and CCL2019, and senior area chair for many conferences. She has given a large number of keynotes/tutorials presentations in Event Extraction, Natural Language Understanding, and Knowledge Base Construction in many conferences including but not limited to ACL, EMNLP, NAACL, NeurIPS, AAAI and KDD.
Email: hengji@illinois.edu
Homepage: `http://blender.cs.illinois.edu/hengji.html`

Yunyao Li is a Principal Research Staff Member and Senior Research Manager with IBM Research - Almaden, where she manages the Scalable Knowledge Intelligence Department. She is a Master Inventor and a member of the IBM Academy of Technology. Her expertise is in the interdisciplinary areas of natural language processing, databases, human-computer interaction, and information retrieval. She is interested in designing, developing, and analyzing large-scale systems that are usable by a wide spectrum of users. Her current research focuses on scalable natural language processing. She regularly gives talks and tutorials at conferences and universities across the globe, including a MOOC on information extraction. She received her Ph.D. from the University of Michigan, Ann Arbor.
Email: yunyaoli@us.ibm.com
Homepage: `https://researcher.watson.ibm.com/researcher/view.php?person=us-yunyaoli`

References

Joost Bastings, Ivan Titov, Wilker Aziz, Diego Marcheggiani, and Khalil Sima'an. 2017. Graph convolutional encoders for syntax-aware neural machine translation. *arXiv preprint arXiv:1704.04675*.

Yu Chen, Lingfei Wu, and Mohammed J Zaki. 2020a. Iterative deep graph learning for graph neural networks: Better and robust node embeddings. In *Proceedings of the 34th Conference on Neural Information Processing Systems*.

Yu Chen, Lingfei Wu, and Mohammed J. Zaki. 2020b. Reinforcement learning based graph-to-sequence model for natural question generation. In *Proceedings of the 8th International Conference on Learning Representations*.

Yu Chen, Lingfei Wu, and Mohammed J Zaki. 2020c. Toward subgraph guided knowledge graph question generation with graph neural networks. *arXiv preprint arXiv:2004.06015*.

Yanlin Feng, Xinyue Chen, Bill Yuchen Lin, Peifeng Wang, Jun Yan, and Xiang Ren. 2020. Scalable multi-hop relational reasoning for knowledge-aware question answering. *arXiv preprint arXiv:2005.00646*.

Will Hamilton, Zhitao Ying, and Jure Leskovec. 2017. Inductive representation learning on large graphs. In *Advances in Neural Information Processing Systems*, pages 1024–1034.

Thomas N Kipf and Max Welling. 2016. Semi-supervised classification with graph convolutional networks. *arXiv preprint arXiv:1609.02907*.

Shucheng Li, Lingfei Wu, Shiwei Feng, Fangli Xu, Fengyuan Xu, and Sheng Zhong. 2020. Graph-to-tree neural networks for learning structured input-output translation with applications to semantic parsing and math word problem. *arXiv preprint arXiv:2004.13781*.

Yujia Li, Daniel Tarlow, Marc Brockschmidt, and Richard Zemel. 2015. Gated graph sequence neural networks. *arXiv preprint arXiv:1511.05493*.

Ying Lin, Heng Ji, Fei Huang, and Lingfei Wu. 2020. A joint neural model for information extraction with global features. In *Proceedings of the 58th Annual Meeting of the Association for Computational Linguistics*, pages 7999–8009.

Kun Xu, Lingfei Wu, Zhiguo Wang, Yansong Feng, Michael Witbrock, and Vadim Sheinin. 2018. Graph2seq: Graph to sequence learning with attention-based neural networks. *arXiv preprint arXiv:1804.00823*.

A Tutorial on Evaluation Metrics used in Natural Language Generation

Mitesh M. Khapra and **Ananya B. Sai**
Robert-Bosch Centre for Data Science & Artificial Intelligence
Indian Institute of Technology Madras
India
{miteshk,ananya}@cse.iitm.ac.in

Abstract

There has been a massive surge of Natural Language Generation (NLG) models in the recent years, accelerated by deep learning and the availability of large-scale datasets. With such rapid progress, it is vital to assess the extent of scientific progress made and identify the areas/components that need improvement. To accomplish this in an automatic and reliable manner, the NLP community has actively pursued the development of automatic evaluation metrics. Especially in the last few years, there has been an increasing focus on evaluation metrics, with several criticisms of existing metrics and proposals for several new metrics. This tutorial presents the evolution of automatic evaluation metrics to their current state along with the emerging trends in this field by specifically addressing the following questions: (i) What makes NLG evaluation challenging? (ii) Why do we need *automatic* evaluation metrics? (iii) What are the existing automatic evaluation metrics and how can they be organised in a coherent taxonomy? (iv) What are the criticisms and shortcomings of existing metrics? (v) What are the possible future directions of research?

1 Tutorial Content Description

Natural Language Generation (NLG) encompasses various tasks that require an automatic generation of human-understandable text such as Machine Translation, Abstractive Summarization, Question Answering, Data-to-text Generation, Dialogue Systems, etc. Each of these tasks has several use-cases with numerous models proposed over the years. The successful application of machine learning and deep learning techniques has transformed the mainstream models for NLG from rule-based systems to data-driven, end-to-end trainable systems. The easier availability of datasets and access to powerful computing resources has led to the wide-spread adoption of these techniques and rapid developments in the field. To track the developments and understand the scientific progress made, these NLG systems need to be evaluated carefully. The ideal way to do so would be to employ expert human evaluators. However, this option would be very time-consuming and expensive, and is thus infeasible. Hence the community has settled for automatic evaluation metrics to track scientific progress in this field.

Automatic Evaluation metrics such as BLEU (Papineni et al., 2002), METEOR (Banerjee and Lavie, 2005), ROUGE (Lin, 2004) have been around for several years and are still predominantly used. They have also been readily adopted for newer tasks in NLG such as Question Generation, Image Captioning, etc, due to the lack of any other relevant metrics. However, there has been heavy criticism for such an adoption of metrics across tasks, corroborated by their poor correlations with human judgements (Liu et al., 2016; Nema and Khapra, 2018; Dhingra et al., 2019). Several new metrics are being proposed to address the shortcomings of the existing ones (Sai et al., 2020b). The emerging metrics also explore the idea of using the context provided for the task (such as a document, image, passage, or tabular data, and so on), unlike BLEU, METEOR, ROUGE, etc. This has lead to the development of 'context-dependent metrics' alongside the 'context-free metrics'.

Both the context-free and context-dependent metrics can be categorized based on their underlying technique into trained metrics and untrained (i.e., rule-based/ heuristic-based) metrics. Untrained metrics can be further classified depending on whether they are word-based (Papineni et al., 2002; Banerjee and Lavie, 2005; Lin, 2004; Snover et al., 2006; Druck and Pang, 2012; Dhingra et al., 2019), character-based (Popovic, 2015; Wang et al., 2016), or embedding-based (Rus and Lintean, 2012; Forgues et al., 2014; Kusner et al., 2015; Mathur et al., 2019; Zhang et al., 2019). Similarly, trained metrics are sub-categorized depending on

Proceedings of NAACL-HLT 2021: Tutorials, pages 15–19
June 6–11, 2021. ©2021 Association for Computational Linguistics

whether they need input features (such as precision, recall, number of words in a sentence, etc,) (Stanojevic and Sima'an, 2014; Ma et al., 2017; Nema and Khapra, 2018) or whether they extract the features from the input sentences in an end-to-end manner (Lowe et al., 2017; Tao et al., 2018; Cui et al., 2018; Shimanaka et al., 2018; Wieting et al., 2019; Sellam et al., 2020; Sai et al., 2020a). In this tutorial, we provide an overview of these different techniques that have been used to formulate automatic evaluation metrics. We also discuss the studies that analyze/inspect these metrics and report their shortcomings. The major criticisms on the metrics include the uninterpretability of the scores (Zhang et al., 2004; Callison-Burch et al., 2006), bias towards specific models (Dusek et al., 2020) or scores (Sai et al., 2019), and their inability to capture all the nuances in a task (Ananthakrishnan et al., 2006). We conclude by presenting the possible next directions of research in automatic evaluation metrics.

1.1 Relevance to computational linguistics community

There is a necessity to compare the myriad of models being proposed for various NLG tasks and scrutinize the progress carefully. Towards this objective, the topic of evaluation metrics has been highly relevant to the linguistics community, in general, and to researchers working on various tasks in NLG, in particular. The number of research papers that critically examine the existing metrics and/or propose new metrics has been rapidly increasing. For example, at least 40 new metrics have been proposed since 2014 for various NLG tasks. We thus believe that the topic of automatic evaluation metrics is garnering more interest in the recent years. This tutorial aims to bring new and existing researchers up-to-speed on the developments related to this topic.

2 Type of the Tutorial

Cutting-edge: This tutorial will follow the growth of automatic evaluation metrics over the years, starting with the initial metrics that are still popularly used today, and building up to the more recent metrics. Substantial emphasis will be given to the recent trends and emerging directions of research on this topic. To the best of our knowledge such a tutorial on evaluation metrics has not been conducted so far in any of the ACL/EACL/IJCNLP/EMNLP/NAACL venues.

3 Tutorial Structure and Schedule Outline

We plan a 3 hour tutorial based on the following content and associated time estimates.

- Introduction (20 min)
  - NLG (A brief history)
  - Have we made progress?
  - Quantifying progress
    - Human/Manual Evaluation
    - Automatic Evaluation
  - Tutorial Roadmap
- Challenges of Automatic Evaluation of NLG tasks (20 min)
  - Breakdown of evaluation criteria for different tasks
    - Machine Translation
    - Abstractive Summarization
    - Question Answering
    - Question Generation
    - Data-to-Text Generation
    - Dialogue Generation
    - Image Captioning
  - Summary of the Challenges
- Taxonomy of Automatic Evaluation Metrics in use (10 min)
  - Context-free v/s Context-dependent metrics
  - Trained metrics v/s Untrained (/heuristic-based) metrics
  - Task-specific v/s Task-agnostic metrics
- Context-free metrics (30 min)
  - Untrained metrics
    - Word or character based metrics
    - Embedding based metrics
  - Trained metrics
    - Feature-based metrics
    - End-to-end trained metrics
- Context-dependent metrics (30 min)
  - Untrained metrics
  - Trained metrics

- Shortcomings identified in existing metrics (40 min)
  - Poor correlations
  - Uninterpretability of scores
  - Bias in the metrics
  - Poor adaptability across tasks
  - Inability to capture all nuances in a task
- Conclusions and future research directions (10 min)

4 Prerequisites

We aim to present the tutorial in a self-contained manner, accommodating audience with various backgrounds. However, it would be helpful to have basic knowledge about Natural Language Processing, Machine Learning, and Deep Learning methods (such as Word embeddings, Recurrent Neural Networks, Sequence-to-sequence models, and Transformers).

5 Presenters

Mitesh M. Khapra, Assistant Professor, Indian Institute of Technology Madras
Email: miteshk@cse.iitm.ac.in
Site: `http://www.cse.iitm.ac.in/~miteshk/`
Mitesh M. Khapra is an Assistant Professor in the Department of Computer Science and Engineering at IIT Madras and is affiliated with the Robert Bosch Centre for Data Science and AI. He co-founded One Fourth Labs, with a mission to design and deliver affordable hands-on courses on AI and related topics. He is also a co-founder of AI4Bharat, a voluntary community with an aim to provide AI-based solutions to India-specific problems. His research interests span the areas of Deep Learning, Multimodal Multilingual Processing, Natural Language Generation, Dialog systems, Question Answering and Indic Language Processing. He has publications in several top conferences and journals including TACL, ACL, NeurIPS, ICLR, EMNLP, EACL, AAAI, etc. He has also served as Area Chair or Senior PC member in top conferences such as ICLR and AAAI. Prior to IIT Madras, he worked as a Researcher at IBM Research India for four and half years. While at IBM, he worked on several interesting problems in the areas of Statistical Machine Translation, Cross Language Learning, Multimodal Learning, Argument Mining and Deep Learning. Prior to IBM, he completed his PhD and M.Tech from IIT Bombay in Jan 2012 and July 2008 respectively. His PhD thesis dealt with the important problem of reusing resources for multilingual computation. During his PhD he was a recipient of the IBM PhD Fellowship (2011) and the Microsoft Rising Star Award (2011). He is also a recipient of the Google Faculty Research Award (2018), the IITM Young Faculty Recognition Award (2019), and the Prof. B. Yegnanarayana Award for Excellence in Research and Teaching (2020). He has previously presented tutorials at NAACL 2016 on "Multilingual Multimodal Language Processing Using Neural Networks" and "Statistical Machine Translation between Related Languages".

Ananya B. Sai, PhD student, Indian Institute of Technology Madras
Email: ananya@cse.iitm.ac.in
Site: `https://ananyasaib.github.io/`
Ananya Sai is currently a PhD student in the Department of Computer Science and Engineering at IIT Madras working with Dr. Mitesh M. Khapra. Her research interests include Natural Language Processing, Deep Learning, Adversarial Attacks, and Dialog Systems. Some of her recent research works are related to adversarial attacks on trained evaluation models. These include whitebox attacks and synthetic or human crafted adversarial modifications of the input sentences to fool the models. She has co-created a multi-reference dialogue dataset and has explored the benefits of task-specific pretraining for evaluating dialogue systems. She is a recipient of Google PhD Fellowship (2019) and the Prime Minister Fellowship for Doctoral Research (2020). She has published papers in TACL, AAAI, and IJCAI.

References

Ananthakrishnan, Pushpak Bhattacharyya, Murugesan Sasikumar, and Ritesh M. Shah. 2006. Some issues in automatic evaluation of english-hindi mt : More blues for BLEU. In *Proceeding of 5th International Conference on Natural Language Processing (ICON-07). Hyderabad, India.*

Satanjeev Banerjee and Alon Lavie. 2005. METEOR: An automatic metric for MT evaluation with improved correlation with human judgments. In *Proceedings of the ACL Workshop on Intrinsic and Extrinsic Evaluation Measures for Machine Translation and/or Summarization*, pages 65–72, Ann Arbor, Michigan. Association for Computational Linguistics.

Chris Callison-Burch, Miles Osborne, and Philipp Koehn. 2006. Re-evaluating the role of Bleu in machine translation research. In *11th Conference of the European Chapter of the Association for Computational Linguistics*, Trento, Italy. Association for Computational Linguistics.

Yin Cui, Guandao Yang, Andreas Veit, Xun Huang, and Serge J. Belongie. 2018. Learning to evaluate image captioning. In *2018 IEEE Conference on Computer Vision and Pattern Recognition, CVPR 2018, Salt Lake City, UT, USA, June 18-22, 2018*, pages 5804–5812. IEEE Computer Society.

Bhuwan Dhingra, Manaal Faruqui, Ankur P. Parikh, Ming-Wei Chang, Dipanjan Das, and William W. Cohen. 2019. Handling divergent reference texts when evaluating table-to-text generation. In *Proceedings of the 57th Conference of the Association for Computational Linguistics, ACL 2019, Florence, Italy, July 28- August 2, 2019, Volume 1: Long Papers*, pages 4884–4895. Association for Computational Linguistics.

Gregory Druck and Bo Pang. 2012. Spice it up? mining refinements to online instructions from user generated content. In *Proceedings of the 50th Annual Meeting of the Association for Computational Linguistics (Volume 1: Long Papers)*, pages 545–553, Jeju Island, Korea. Association for Computational Linguistics.

Ondrej Dusek, Jekaterina Novikova, and Verena Rieser. 2020. Evaluating the state-of-the-art of end-to-end natural language generation: The E2E NLG challenge. *Comput. Speech Lang.*, 59:123–156.

Gabriel Forgues, Joelle Pineau, Jean-Marie Larchevêque, and Réal Tremblay. 2014. Bootstrapping dialog systems with word embeddings. In *Neurips, modern machine learning and natural language processing workshop*, volume 2.

Matt J. Kusner, Yu Sun, Nicholas I. Kolkin, and Kilian Q. Weinberger. 2015. From word embeddings to document distances. In *Proceedings of the 32nd International Conference on Machine Learning, ICML 2015, Lille, France, 6-11 July 2015*, volume 37 of *JMLR Workshop and Conference Proceedings*, pages 957–966. JMLR.org.

Chin-Yew Lin. 2004. ROUGE: A package for automatic evaluation of summaries. In *Text Summarization Branches Out*, pages 74–81, Barcelona, Spain. Association for Computational Linguistics.

Chia-Wei Liu, Ryan Lowe, Iulian Serban, Michael Noseworthy, Laurent Charlin, and Joelle Pineau. 2016. How NOT to evaluate your dialogue system: An empirical study of unsupervised evaluation metrics for dialogue response generation. In *Proceedings of the 2016 Conference on Empirical Methods in Natural Language Processing, EMNLP 2016, Austin, Texas, USA, November 1-4, 2016*, pages 2122–2132. The Association for Computational Linguistics.

Ryan Lowe, Michael Noseworthy, Iulian Vlad Serban, Nicolas Angelard-Gontier, Yoshua Bengio, and Joelle Pineau. 2017. Towards an automatic turing test: Learning to evaluate dialogue responses. In *Proceedings of the 55th Annual Meeting of the Association for Computational Linguistics, ACL 2017, Vancouver, Canada, July 30 - August 4, Volume 1: Long Papers*, pages 1116–1126. Association for Computational Linguistics.

Qingsong Ma, Yvette Graham, Shugen Wang, and Qun Liu. 2017. Blend: a novel combined MT metric based on direct assessment - CASICT-DCU submission to WMT17 metrics task. In *Proceedings of the Second Conference on Machine Translation, WMT 2017, Copenhagen, Denmark, September 7-8, 2017*, pages 598–603. Association for Computational Linguistics.

Nitika Mathur, Timothy Baldwin, and Trevor Cohn. 2019. Putting evaluation in context: Contextual embeddings improve machine translation evaluation. In *Proceedings of the 57th Conference of the Association for Computational Linguistics, ACL 2019, Florence, Italy, July 28- August 2, 2019, Volume 1: Long Papers*, pages 2799–2808. Association for Computational Linguistics.

Preksha Nema and Mitesh M. Khapra. 2018. Towards a better metric for evaluating question generation systems. In *Proceedings of the 2018 Conference on Empirical Methods in Natural Language Processing, Brussels, Belgium, October 31 - November 4, 2018*, pages 3950–3959. Association for Computational Linguistics.

Kishore Papineni, Salim Roukos, Todd Ward, and Wei-Jing Zhu. 2002. Bleu: a method for automatic evaluation of machine translation. In *Proceedings of the 40th Annual Meeting of the Association for Computational Linguistics*, pages 311–318, Philadelphia, Pennsylvania, USA. Association for Computational Linguistics.

Maja Popovic. 2015. chrf: character n-gram f-score for automatic MT evaluation. In *Proceedings of the Tenth Workshop on Statistical Machine Translation, WMT@EMNLP 2015, 17-18 September 2015, Lisbon, Portugal*, pages 392–395. The Association for Computer Linguistics.

Vasile Rus and Mihai C. Lintean. 2012. A comparison of greedy and optimal assessment of natural language student input using word-to-word similarity metrics. In *BEA@NAACL-HLT*.

Ananya B. Sai, Mithun Das Gupta, Mitesh M. Khapra, and Mukundhan Srinivasan. 2019. Re-evaluating ADEM: A deeper look at scoring dialogue responses. In *The Thirty-Third AAAI Conference on Artificial*

Intelligence, AAAI 2019, The Thirty-First Innovative Applications of Artificial Intelligence Conference, IAAI 2019, The Ninth AAAI Symposium on Educational Advances in Artificial Intelligence, EAAI 2019, Honolulu, Hawaii, USA, January 27 - February 1, 2019, pages 6220–6227. AAAI Press.

Ananya B. Sai, Akash Kumar Mohankumar, Siddhartha Arora, and Mitesh M. Khapra. 2020a. Improving dialog evaluation with a multi-reference adversarial dataset and large scale pretraining. *Trans. Assoc. Comput. Linguistics*, 8:810–827.

Ananya B. Sai, Akash Kumar Mohankumar, and Mitesh M. Khapra. 2020b. A survey of evaluation metrics used for NLG systems. *CoRR*, abs/2008.12009.

Thibault Sellam, Dipanjan Das, and Ankur P. Parikh. 2020. BLEURT: learning robust metrics for text generation. *CoRR*, abs/2004.04696.

Hiroki Shimanaka, Tomoyuki Kajiwara, and Mamoru Komachi. 2018. RUSE: regressor using sentence embeddings for automatic machine translation evaluation. In *Proceedings of the Third Conference on Machine Translation: Shared Task Papers, WMT 2018, Belgium, Brussels, October 31 - November 1, 2018*, pages 751–758. Association for Computational Linguistics.

Matthew Snover, Bonnie Dorr, Richard Schwartz, Linnea Micciulla, and John Makhoul. 2006. A study of translation edit rate with targeted human annotation. In *In Proceedings of Association for Machine Translation in the Americas*, pages 223–231.

Milos Stanojevic and Khalil Sima'an. 2014. Fitting sentence level translation evaluation with many dense features. In *Proceedings of the 2014 Conference on Empirical Methods in Natural Language Processing, EMNLP 2014, October 25-29, 2014, Doha, Qatar, A meeting of SIGDAT, a Special Interest Group of the ACL*, pages 202–206. ACL.

Chongyang Tao, Lili Mou, Dongyan Zhao, and Rui Yan. 2018. RUBER: an unsupervised method for automatic evaluation of open-domain dialog systems. In *Proceedings of the Thirty-Second AAAI Conference on Artificial Intelligence, (AAAI-18), the 30th innovative Applications of Artificial Intelligence (IAAI-18), and the 8th AAAI Symposium on Educational Advances in Artificial Intelligence (EAAI-18), New Orleans, Louisiana, USA, February 2-7, 2018*, pages 722–729. AAAI Press.

Weiyue Wang, Jan-Thorsten Peter, Hendrik Rosendahl, and Hermann Ney. 2016. Character: Translation edit rate on character level. In *Proceedings of the First Conference on Machine Translation, WMT 2016, colocated with ACL 2016, August 11-12, Berlin, Germany*, pages 505–510. The Association for Computer Linguistics.

John Wieting, Taylor Berg-Kirkpatrick, Kevin Gimpel, and Graham Neubig. 2019. Beyond BLEU: training neural machine translation with semantic similarity. In *Proceedings of the 57th Conference of the Association for Computational Linguistics, ACL 2019, Florence, Italy, July 28- August 2, 2019, Volume 1: Long Papers*, pages 4344–4355. Association for Computational Linguistics.

Tianyi Zhang, Varsha Kishore, Felix Wu, Kilian Q. Weinberger, and Yoav Artzi. 2019. Bertscore: Evaluating text generation with bert. *ArXiv*, abs/1904.09675.

Ying Zhang, Stephan Vogel, and Alex Waibel. 2004. Interpreting BLEU/NIST scores: How much improvement do we need to have a better system? In *Proceedings of the Fourth International Conference on Language Resources and Evaluation, LREC 2004, May 26-28, 2004, Lisbon, Portugal*. European Language Resources Association.

Beyond Paragraphs: NLP for Long Sequences

Iz Beltagy[†] **Arman Cohan**[†] **Hannaneh Hajishirzi**[‡] **Sewon Min**[‡] **Matthew E. Peters**[†]
[‡] Paul G. Allen School, University of Washington, Seattle, WA
[†] Allen Institute for AI, Seattle, WA

1 Introduction

A significant subset of natural language data includes documents that span thousands of tokens. The ability to process such long sequences is critical for many NLP tasks including document classification, summarization, multi-hop, and open-domain question answering, and document-level or multi-document relationship extraction and coreference resolution. These tasks have important practical applications in domains such as scientific document understanding and the digital humanities (Ammar et al., 2018; Cohan et al., 2018; Kociský et al., 2018; Lo et al., 2020; Wang et al., 2020a). Yet, scaling state-of-the-art models to long sequences is challenging as many models are designed and tested for shorter sequences. One notable example is transformer models (Vaswani et al., 2017) that have $O(N^2)$ computational cost in the sequence length N, making them prohibitively expensive to run for many long sequence tasks. This is reflected in many widely-used models such as RoBERTa and BERT where the sequence length is limited to only 512 tokens.

In this tutorial, we aim at bringing interested NLP researchers up to speed about the recent and ongoing techniques for document-level representation learning. Additionally, our goal is to reveal new research opportunities to the audience, which will hopefully bring us closer to address existing challenges in this domain.

We will first provide an overview of established long sequence NLP techniques, including hierarchical, graph-based, and retrieval-based methods. We will then focus on the recent long-sequence transformer methods, how they compare to each other, and how they can be applied to NLP tasks (see Tay et al. (2020) for a recent survey). We will also discuss various memory-saving methods that are key to processing long sequences. Throughout the tutorial, we will use classification, question answering, and information extraction as motivating tasks. In the end, we will have a hands-on coding exercise focused on summarization.[1]

2 Description

Tutorial Content This tutorial covers methods for long-sequence processing and their application to NLP tasks. We will start by explaining why processing long sequences is difficult. Many popular models scale poorly with the sequence length, either in computational or memory requirements, making them too expensive or impossible to run on current hardware. Another reason is that we want models that can capture long-distance information while ignoring large amounts of irrelevant text. The introduction also covers the tasks that we will use throughout the tutorial, namely information extraction (relation extraction (Jia et al., 2019) and coreference resolution (Pradhan et al., 2012; Bamman et al., 2020)), question answering (especially the multi-hop setting as in HotpotQA (Yang et al., 2018) and Wikihop (Welbl et al., 2018)), and document classification, and summarization.

The next section will review well-established methods for dealing with long sequences, namely chunking and graph based methods. Chunking refers to splitting the sequence into smaller chunks, processing each one independently, then aggregating them in a task-specific way (Joshi et al., 2019). Hierarchical models are a special case of chunking where the chunks are linguistic constructs (usually sentences) that are aggregated following the document hierarchy (Yang et al., 2016). Finally, retrieval-based methods use a recall-optimized simple model to retrieve short text snippets relevant for the task, then follow up with a stronger, more

[1] Slides and Code `https://github.com/allenai/naacl2021-longdoc-tutorial`

Proceedings of NAACL-HLT 2021: Tutorials, pages 20–24
June 6–11, 2021.

expensive model. Retrieval methods have been discussed in detail in the Open Domain QA tutorial (Chen and Yih, 2020) so we will cover it here very briefly. Graph-based methods will also be discussed, with a focus on question answering. These methods usually use local context to identify potentially relevant information across the document, heuristically connect the identified information in a graph, then apply a graph neural network (Kipf and Welling, 2017) to propagate information across the document between the snippets. This is particularly effective for the multi-hop reasoning setting (Fang et al., 2019).

Next, we will focus on the recent transformer-based methods for efficient processing of long sequences. The key question these models are addressing is how to perform the expensive $O(N^2)$ self-attention computation efficiently. All models make this computation faster by approximating the full self-attention leading to different models with different behaviors and applications. We will survey a few of the key papers summarized in Tay et al. (2020). In particular, we will talk about Transformer-XL (Dai et al., 2019), Longformer (Beltagy et al., 2020), Reformer (Kitaev et al., 2020) and Linformer (Wang et al., 2020b). We will also discuss how they apply to NLP tasks; Transformer-XL is mainly suitable for autoregressive tasks while the other three are equally suitable for autoregressive and bidirectional tasks. We will compare the performance of the other three models on various NLP tasks.

The next section discusses pretraining and finetuning of the transformer models. For pretraining, we will discuss different approaches to warm start the model weights from existing pretrained models for short sequences (Gupta and Berant, 2020; Beltagy et al., 2020). These approaches are versatile and make it possible to adapt most existing pretrained transformer models for short sequences into models that can process long sequences with a tiny pretraining cost. We will also demonstrate how to finetune such models for tasks such as question answering and classification.

The following section is a practical use case on summarization. We will show how to start from the BART (Lewis et al., 2020) checkpoint, convert it into a model that can work with a long input that's tens of thousands of tokens long, then finetune it on a long-input summarization task. It will also discuss practical techniques necessary to run the model on current hardware, including memory optimization techniques such as gradient checkpointing (Chen et al., 2016) and gradient accumulation. These are generic memory saving methods applicable to all neural models, and especially applicable in the long sequence setting.

Finally, the future work section will discuss open questions and future research directions like pretraining objectives that are better suited for long documents, encoder-decoder models with long output sequence, the balance between two-stage retrieval methods and single stage methods with long input, and how we think about long-sequence scaling for large models where the self-attention compute overhead reduces relative to feed-forward layers.

Relevance to ACL The models we cover are generic machine learning tools, but we discuss them from the NLP perspective, and study their application to core NLP tasks like IE, QA, and text generation. These methods have the potential to improve tasks that are currently challenging like multi-document summarization, story generation, and long dialogues. It can also enable new applications that have not yet been considered.

3 Type of the tutorial

This is a **cutting-edge** tutorial. The methods we discuss, especially the transformer-based and the graph-based methods, are active areas of research.

4 Outline

This tutorial will be 3 hours long.

1. **Introduction** (15 minutes long): This section will introduce the theme of the tutorial: why processing long sequence is important and why it is difficult. It will also introduce the NLP end-tasks that we will use throughout the tutorial.

2. **Chunking, hierarchical, and graph based methods** (35 minutes long): This section discusses graph-based methods and their application to information extraction and question answering, especially in the multi-hop reasoning setting. It also covers chunking and hierarchical methods as applied to coreference resolution, classification, and question answering.

3. **Transformer-based methods** (45 minutes long): This section reviews recently introduced long-sequence transformer models, compares the pros and cons of their designs, and discuss their applicability to NLP applications.

4. **Pretraining and finetuning** (25 minutes long): This section discusses how the long-sequence transformer methods are pretrained and how they are finetuned for downstream tasks including classification and question answering.

5. **Use Case: Summarization** (40 minutes long): This section is a practical exercise where we demonstrate in code how to build and train a long-document summarization model. It will also cover the technical details of multiple memory-saving methods that are key for training models on long sequences including gradient accumulation, and gradient checkpointing.

6. **Open problems and directions** (20 minutes long): In this final section, we will provide an outlook into the future. We will highlight both open problems and point to future research directions.

5 Breadth

We estimate 75% of the work covered will not be by the tutorial presenters.

6 Prerequisites

- Machine Learning: Basic knowledge of common recent neural network architectures like RNNs, and Transformers.
- Computational linguistics: Familiarity with standard NLP tasks such as text classification, natural language generation, and question answering.

7 Reading List

Reading the following papers is nice to have but not required for attendance.

- Hierarchical attention for classification (Yang et al., 2016)
- Graph network for question answering (Fang et al., 2019)
- Survey of long sequence transformers (Tay et al., 2020)
- Extractive/Abstractive summarization (Subramanian et al., 2019)

8 Instructors

In alphabetical order,

Iz Beltagy Iz Beltagy is a Research Scientist at AI2 focusing on language modeling, domain adaptation, and document-level understanding. His research has been recognized with a best paper honorary mention at ACL 2020. He worked as a Teaching Assistant at the University of Texas at Austin teaching computer science courses.
Email: `beltagy@allenai.org`
Homepage: `beltagy.net`

Arman Cohan Arman Cohan is a Research Scientist at AI2 focusing on representation learning and transfer learning methods, as well as NLP applications in scientific and health-related domains. His research has been recognized with a best paper award at EMNLP 2017, an honorable mention at COLING 2018, and Harold N. Glassman Distinguished Doctoral Dissertation award in 2019.
Email: `armanc@allenai.org`
Homepage: `armancohan.com`

Hannaneh Hajishirzi Hannaneh Hajishirzi is an Assistant Professor in the Paul G. Allen School of Computer Science & Engineering at the University of Washington and a Research Fellow at the Allen Institute for AI. Her research spans different areas in NLP, focusing on developing machine learning algorithms that represent, comprehend, and reason about textual data at large scale. Honors include the Sloan Fellowship, Allen Distinguished Investigator Award, Intel rising star award, multiple best paper and honorable mention awards, and several industry research faculty awards. She has given previous tutorials at top NLP conferences.
Email: `hannaneh@cs.washington.edu`
Homepage: `homes.cs.washington.edu/~hannaneh/`

Sewon Min Sewon Min is a Ph.D. student in the Paul G. Allen School of Computer Science & Engineering at the University of Washington, advised by Hannaneh Hajishirzi and Luke Zettlemoyer. Her research focuses on natural language understanding, question answering, and knowledge representation.

She is a co-organizer of the 3rd Workshop on Machine Reading for Question Answering at EMNLP 2021, Competition on Efficient Open-domain Question Answering at NeurIPS 2020, and Workshop on Structured and Unstructured KBs at AKBC 2020.
Email: sewon@cs.washington.edu
Homepage: shmsw25.github.io

Matthew Peters Matthew Peters is a Research Scientist at AI2 focusing on representation learning for NLP, transfer methods, and model interpretability. His research was awarded a best paper at NAACL-HLT 2018, and he gave a previous tutorial at NAACL-HLT 2019.
Email: matthewp@allenai.org
Homepage: scholar.google.com/citations?user=K5nCPZwAAAAJ

9 Estimated Attendance

Due to the broad appeal, we expect the tutorial to be well attended with around 150 people. This is especially the case for the long-sequence transformer methods because they open up pretrained models to applications that haven't been considered before. They are also easy to use, something that appeals to researchers and practitioners alike.

This tutorial has not been previously offered, but some of the methods have been covered before. In particular, retrieval-based methods have been covered in the Open-Domain QA tutorial at ACL 2020 (Chen and Yih, 2020), so we won't cover this topic and will refer the attendees to the previous tutorial.

10 Venue

The tutorial will be held at NAACL-HLT 2021.

11 Open Access

All the slides, video recordings, and software used for the tutorial will be publicly available.

References

Waleed Ammar, Dirk Groeneveld, Chandra Bhagavatula, Iz Beltagy, Miles Crawford, Doug Downey, Jason Dunkelberger, Ahmed Elgohary, Sergey Feldman, Vu Ha, Rodney Kinney, Sebastian Kohlmeier, Kyle Lo, Tyler Murray, Hsu-Han Ooi, Matthew Peters, Joanna Power, Sam Skjonsberg, Lucy Wang, Chris Wilhelm, Zheng Yuan, Madeleine van Zuylen, and Oren Etzioni. 2018. Construction of the literature graph in semantic scholar. In *NAACL-HLT*.

David Bamman, Olivia Lewke, and Anya Mansoor. 2020. An annotated dataset of coreference in english literature. In *LREC*.

Iz Beltagy, Matthew E. Peters, and Arman Cohan. 2020. Longformer: The long-document transformer. *ArXiv*, abs/2004.05150.

Danqi Chen and Wen-tau Yih. 2020. Open-domain question answering. In *Proceedings of the 58th Annual Meeting of the Association for Computational Linguistics: Tutorial Abstracts*, pages 34–37, Online. Association for Computational Linguistics.

Tianqi Chen, Bing Xu, Chiyuan Zhang, and Carlos Guestrin. 2016. Training deep nets with sublinear memory cost. *arXiv preprint*, abs/1604.06174.

Arman Cohan, Franck Dernoncourt, Doo Soon Kim, Trung Bui, Seokhwan Kim, Walter Chang, and Nazli Goharian. 2018. A discourse-aware attention model for abstractive summarization of long documents. In *NAACL-HLT*.

Zihang Dai, Zhilin Yang, Yiming Yang, Jaime G. Carbonell, Quoc V. Le, and Ruslan Salakhutdinov. 2019. Transformer-XL: Attentive language models beyond a fixed-length context. In *ACL*.

Yuwei Fang, Siqi Sun, Zhe Gan, Rohit Pillai, Shuohang Wang, and Jing jing Liu. 2019. Hierarchical graph network for multi-hop question answering. *arXiv preprint*, abs/1911.03631.

Ankit Gupta and Jonathan Berant. 2020. Gmat: Global memory augmentation for transformers. *ArXiv*, abs/2006.03274.

Robin Jia, Cliff Wong, and Hoifung Poon. 2019. Document-level n-ary relation extraction with multi-scale representation learning. In *Proceedings of the 2019 Conference of the North American Chapter of the Association for Computational Linguistics: Human Language Technologies, Volume 1 (Long and Short Papers)*.

Mandar Joshi, Omer Levy, Luke Zettlemoyer, and Daniel Weld. 2019. BERT for coreference resolution: Baselines and analysis. In *EMNLP-IJCNLP*.

Thomas N Kipf and Max Welling. 2017. Semi-supervised classification with graph convolutional networks. *ICLR*.

Nikita Kitaev, Lukasz Kaiser, and Anselm Levskaya. 2020. Reformer: The efficient transformer. In *ICLR*.

Tomás Kociský, Jonathan Schwarz, P. Blunsom, Chris Dyer, K. Hermann, Gábor Melis, and Edward Grefenstette. 2018. The narrativeqa reading comprehension challenge. *Transactions of the Association for Computational Linguistics*, 6:317–328.

Mike Lewis, Yinhan Liu, Naman Goyal, Marjan Ghazvininejad, Abdelrahman Mohamed, Omer Levy, Veselin Stoyanov, and Luke Zettlemoyer. 2020. BART: Denoising sequence-to-sequence pre-training for natural language generation, translation, and comprehension. In *Proceedings of the 58th Annual Meeting of the Association for Computational Linguistics*, pages 7871–7880, Online. Association for Computational Linguistics.

Kyle Lo, Lucy Lu Wang, Mark Neumann, Rodney Kinney, and Daniel Weld. 2020. S2ORC: The semantic scholar open research corpus. In *ACL*.

Sameer Pradhan, Alessandro Moschitti, Nianwen Xue, Olga Uryupina, and Yuchen Zhang. 2012. CoNLL-2012 shared task: Modeling multilingual unrestricted coreference in OntoNotes. In *Joint Conference on EMNLP and CoNLL - Shared Task*, pages 1–40, Jeju Island, Korea. Association for Computational Linguistics.

Sandeep Subramanian, Raymond Li, Jonathan Pilault, and C. Pal. 2019. On extractive and abstractive neural document summarization with transformer language models. *ArXiv*, abs/1909.03186.

Yi Tay, Mostafa Dehghani, Dara Bahri, and Donald Metzler. 2020. Efficient transformers: A survey. *ArXiv*, abs/2009.06732.

Ashish Vaswani, Noam Shazeer, Niki Parmar, Jakob Uszkoreit, Llion Jones, Aidan N. Gomez, Lukasz Kaiser, and Illia Polosukhin. 2017. Attention is all you need. In *NIPS*.

Lucy Lu Wang, Kyle Lo, Yoganand Chandrasekhar, Russell Reas, Jiangjiang Yang, Darrin Eide, Kathryn Funk, Rodney Kinney, Ziyang Liu, William Merrill, et al. 2020a. Cord-19: The covid-19 open research dataset. *ArXiv*.

Sinong Wang, Belinda Li, Madian Khabsa, Han Fang, and Hao Ma. 2020b. Linformer: Self-attention with linear complexity. *arXiv preprint arXiv:2006.04768*.

Johannes Welbl, Pontus Stenetorp, and Sebastian Riedel. 2018. Constructing datasets for multi-hop reading comprehension across documents. *TACL*, 6:287–302.

Zhilin Yang, Peng Qi, Saizheng Zhang, Yoshua Bengio, William W. Cohen, Ruslan Salakhutdinov, and Christopher D. Manning. 2018. HotpotQA: A dataset for diverse, explainable multi-hop question answering. In *EMNLP*.

Zichao Yang, Diyi Yang, Chris Dyer, Xiaodong He, Alex Smola, and Eduard Hovy. 2016. Hierarchical attention networks for document classification. In *Proceedings of the 2016 Conference of the North American Chapter of the Association for Computational Linguistics: Human Language Technologies*, pages 1480–1489, San Diego, California. Association for Computational Linguistics.

Crowdsourcing Natural Language Data at Scale: A Hands-On Tutorial

Alexey Drutsa
Yandex
Moscow, Russia

Dmitry Ustalov
Yandex
Saint Petersburg, Russia

Valentina Fedorova
Yandex
Moscow, Russia

{adrutsa,dustalov,valya17}@yandex-team.ru

Olga Megorskaya
Yandex
Saint Petersburg, Russia
omegorskaya@yandex-team.ru

Daria Baidakova
Yandex
Moscow, Russia
dbaidakova@yandex-team.ru

Abstract

In this tutorial, we present a portion of unique industry experience in efficient natural language data annotation via crowdsourcing shared by both leading researchers and engineers from Yandex. We will make an introduction to data labeling via public crowdsourcing marketplaces and will present the key components of efficient label collection. This will be followed by a practical session, where participants address a real-world language resource production task, experiment with selecting settings for the labeling process, and launch their label collection project on one of the largest crowdsourcing marketplaces. The projects will be run on real crowds within the tutorial session and we will present useful quality control techniques and provide the attendees with an opportunity to discuss their own annotation ideas.

Tutorial Type: Introductory

1 Description

Training and evaluating modern Natural Language Processing (NLP) models require large-scale multilingual language resources of high quality. Traditionally, such resources have been created by groups of experts or by using automated silver standards. Crowdsourcing has become a popular approach for data labeling that allows annotating language resources in a shorter time and at a lower cost than the experts while maintaining expert-level result quality. Examples include Search Relevance Evaluation, Machine Translation, Question Answering, Corpus Annotation, etc. However, for running crowdsourcing successfully, it is essential to pay attention to task design, quality control, and annotator incentives. This tutorial aims to teach attendees how to efficiently use crowdsourcing for annotating language resources on a large scale. The tutorial is composed of

1. a theoretical part aimed at explaining the methodology for labeling process in crowdsourcing and main algorithms required to obtain high-quality data (including aggregation, incremental relabeling, and quality-dependent pricing), and

2. practice sessions for setting up and running language resource annotation project on one of the largest public crowdsourcing marketplaces.

The goals of our tutorial are to explain the fundamental techniques for aggregation, incremental relabeling, and pricing in connection to each other and to teach attendees the main principles for setting up an efficient process of language resource annotation on a crowdsourcing marketplace. We will share our best practices and allow the attendees to discuss their issues with language data labeling with crowdsourcing.

To establish trust and allow the attendees to evaluate the crowdsourced results even after the tutorial carefully, we decide to use English as the language of our tutorial datasets. According to our six years of experience, we would emphasize that the same techniques can successfully apply to virtually any language and domain that the crowd performers command, including Russian, Turkish, Vietnamese, and many other languages. The opportunity to attract crowd performers from under-represented languages, backgrounds, and demographics brings the possibility to create more useful language resources and evaluate NLP systems fairly in more challenging multilingual setups.

Proceedings of NAACL-HLT 2021: Tutorials, pages 25–30
June 6–11, 2021.

1.1 Introduction to Crowdsourcing

We will start with an *introduction* that includes crowdsourcing terminology and examples of tasks on crowdsourcing marketplaces. We will also demonstrate why crowdsourcing is becoming more popular in working with data on a large scale, showing successful crowdsourcing applications for language resource development, and describing current industry trends of crowdsourcing use.

1.2 Key Components for Efficient Data Collection

We will discuss thoroughly *the key components* required to collect labeled data: proper decomposition of tasks (construction of a pipeline of several small tasks instead of one large human intelligent task), easy to read and follow task instructions, easy to use task interfaces, quality control techniques, an overview of aggregation methods, and pricing.

Quality control techniques include approaches "before" task performance (selection of performers, education and exam tasks), the ones "during" task performance (golden sets, motivation of performers, tricks to remove bots and cheaters), and approaches "after" task performance (post verification/acceptance, consensus between performers).

We will share best practices, including critical aspects and pitfalls when designing instructions & interfaces for performers, vital settings in different types of templates, training, and examination for performers selection, pipelines for evaluating the labeling process. Also, we will demonstrate typical crowdsourcing pipelines used in industrial applications, including Machine Translation, Content Moderation, Named Entity Recognition, etc.

1.3 Hands-on Crowdsourcing Practice

We will conduct *a hands-on practice session*, which is the vital and the longest part of our tutorial. We will encourage the attendees to apply the techniques, and best practices learned during the first part of the tutorial. For this purpose, we propose the attendees run their own crowdsourced Spoken Language Recognition pipeline on actual crowd performers. As the *input* the attendees have audio files of variable quality in English, as the *output* they should provide high-quality transcriptions for these recordings obtained via crowdsourcing. Each attendee will be involved in brainstorming the suitable crowdsourcing pipeline for the given task and configuring and launching the annotation project online on the real crowd while optimizing quality and cost.

Since creating a project from scratch might be time-consuming, we will propose our attendees choose from the most popular pre-installed templates (text input or audio playback). We will also provide the attendees with pre-paid accounts and data sets for annotation. By the end of the practice session, the attendees will learn to construct a functional pipeline for data collection and labeling, become familiar with one of the largest crowdsourcing marketplaces, and launch projects independently.

1.4 Advanced Techniques

We will discuss *the major theoretical results*, computational techniques and ideas which improve the quality of crowdsourcing annotations, and *summarize the open research questions on the topic.*

Crowd Consensus Methods. Classical models: Majority Vote, Dawid-Skene (Dawid and Skene, 1979), GLAD (Whitehill et al., 2009), Minimax Entropy (Zhou et al., 2015). Analysis of aggregation performance and difficulties in comparing aggregation models in unsupervised setting (Sheshadri and Lease, 2013; Imamura et al., 2018). Advanced works on aggregation: combination of aggregation and learning a classifier (Raykar et al., 2010), using features of tasks and performers for aggregation (Ruvolo et al., 2013; Welinder et al., 2010; Jin et al., 2017), aggregation of crowdsourced pairwise comparisons (Chen et al., 2013) and texts (Li and Fukumoto, 2019).

Incremental Relabeling (IRL). Motivation and the problem of incremental relabeling: IRL based on Majority Vote; IRL methods with worker quality scores (Ipeirotis et al., 2014; Ertekin et al., 2012; Abraham et al., 2016); active learning (Lin et al., 2014). Connections between aggregation and IRL algorithms. Experimental results of using IRL at crowdsourcing marketplaces.

Task Pricing. Practical approaches for task pricing (Wang et al., 2013; Cheng et al., 2015; Yin et al., 2013). Theoretical background for pricing mechanisms in crowdsourcing: efficiency, stability, incentive compatibility, etc. Pricing experiments and industrial experience of using pricing at crowdsourcing platforms.

Task Design for NLP. Most crowdsourcing tasks are domain-specific (Callison-Burch and Dredze,

2010; Biemann, 2013) and designed manually, yet the task design can be made more efficient by using the generic workflow patterns (Bernstein et al., 2010; Gadiraju et al., 2019), computer-supported methods (Little et al., 2009), and crowd-supported methods (Bragg et al., 2018).

1.5 Concluding Remarks

Finally, we will finish with analyzing obtained results from the launched projects. This step demonstrates the process of verification of collected data. Together with the attendees, we will discuss which aggregation algorithms can be applied, analyze outcome label distribution, check performer quality and contribution, elaborate on budget control, detect possible anomalies and problems. We will then share practical advice, discuss pitfalls and possible solutions, ask the attendees for feedback on the learning progress, and answer final questions.

By the end of the tutorial, attendees will be familiar with

- key components required to produce language resources via crowdsourcing efficiently;
- state-of-the-art techniques to control the annotation quality and to aggregate the annotation results;
- advanced methods that allow to balance out between the quality and costs;
- practice of creating, configuring, and running data collection projects on real performers on one of the largest global crowdsourcing platforms.

2 Outline

Our tutorial includes the following sessions:

- Introduction to Crowdsourcing (15 min)
- Key Components for Efficient Data Collection (30 min)
- Practice Session I (60 min)
- Lunch Break (45 min)
- Advanced Techniques (45 min)
- Practice Session II (30 min)
- Results Evaluation and Concluding Remarks (15 min)

3 Prerequisites for the Attendees

We expect that our tutorial will address an audience with a wide range of backgrounds and interests. Thus, even a beginner, each participant will be able to practice their skills in producing language resources via a crowdsourcing marketplace (this practical part will constitute most of our tutorial timeline).

Our tutorial contains an introduction that positions the topic among related areas and gives the necessary knowledge to understand the main components of data labeling processes. Thus, the entry threshold is shallow to start learning and understanding the topic. Only minimal knowledge on collecting labels is required: no knowledge on crowdsourcing, aggregation, incremental relabeling, and pricing is needed.

We plan to share rich experiences of constructing and applying large-scale data collection pipelines while highlighting the best practices and pitfalls. As a result, any person who develops a web service or a software product based on labeled data and NLP will learn how to construct a language data annotation pipeline, obtain high-quality labels under a limited budget, and avoid common pitfalls.

4 Reading List

We offer an optional reading list for the tutorial attendees. These references allow one to understand crowdsourcing annotation basics for maximizing the learning outcomes from our hands-on tutorial. We will nevertheless cover these materials during the workshop.

Quality Control. Dawid and Skene (1979); Li and Fukumoto (2019)

Task Design for NLP. Bernstein et al. (2010); Callison-Burch and Dredze (2010); Biemann (2013)

Incentives. Snow et al. (2008); Wang et al. (2013)

5 Tutorial Presenters

Alexey Drutsa (PhD), Yandex

Alexey is responsible for data-driven decisions and the ecosystem of Toloka, the open global crowd platform. His research interests are focused on Machine Learning, Data Analysis, Auction Theory; his research is published at ICML, NeurIPS, WSDM, WWW, KDD, SIGIR, CIKM, and TWEB.

Alexey is a co-author of three tutorials on practical A/B testing (at KDD '18, WWW '18, and SIGIR '19), five hands-on tutorials on efficient crowdsourcing (at KDD '19, WSDM '20, SIGMOD '20, CVPR '20, and WWW '21), and a co-organizer of the crowdsourcing workshop at NeurIPS2020. He served as a senior PC member at WWW '19 and as a PC member at several NeurIPS, ICML, ICLR, KDD, WSDM, CIKM, and WWW conferences; he was also a session chair at WWW '17. He graduated from Lomonosov Moscow State University (Faculty of Mechanics and Mathematics) in 2008 and received his PhD in Computational Mathematics from the same university in 2011.

🔗 https://research.yandex.com/people/603399

✉ mailto:adrutsa@yandex-team.ru

Dmitry Ustalov (PhD), Yandex

Dmitry is responsible for crowdsourcing studies and product metrics at Toloka. His research, focused on Natural Language Processing and Crowdsourcing, has been published at COLI, ACL, EACL, EMNLP, and LREC. He has been co-organizing the TextGraphs workshop at EMNLP, COLING, and NAACL-HLT since 2019 and the crowdsourcing workshops at NeurIPS and VLDB since 2020. Dmitry teaches quality control in the crowdsourcing course at the Yandex School of Data Analysis and Computer Science Center. He was also a co-author of the crowdsourcing tutorials at WWW '21, SIGMOD '20, and WSDM '20. Dmitry received a bachelor's and master's degrees from the Ural Federal University (Russia), PhD in Computer Science from the South Ural State University (Russia), and post-doctoral training from the University of Mannheim (Germany).

🔗 https://scholar.google.com/citations?user=wPD4g7AAAAAJ

✉ mailto:dustalov@yandex-team.ru

Valentina Fedorova (PhD), Yandex

Valentina is a research analyst at the Crowdsourcing Department of Yandex. She works on research in Crowdsourcing, including aggregation models and algorithms for incremental labeling. Her research has been presented at ICML, NIPS, KDD, SIGIR, and WSDM. She is a co-author of tutorials on crowdsourcing at SIGMOD '20, WSDM '20, and KDD '19. Valentina graduated from Lomonosov Moscow State University (Faculty of Applied Mathematics and Computer Science) and obtained her PhD in Machine Learning from Royal Holloway University of London in 2014. She is reading lectures on response aggregation and IRL for the crowdsourcing course at the Yandex School of Data Analysis (Moscow, Russia) and Computer Science Center (Saint Petersburg, Russia).

🔗 https://research.yandex.com/people/603772

✉ mailto:valya17@yandex-team.ru

Olga Megorskaya, Yandex

Olga Megorskaya, CEO of Toloka. Under Olga's leadership, Toloka platform has grown the number of crowd performers involved in data labeling from several dozen in 2009 up to 4.1 million in 2020 and became a global infrastructure for data labeling available for all ML specialists. Olga is responsible for providing human-labeled data for all AI projects at Yandex. She is in charge of integrating crowdsourcing into other business processes, such as customer support, product localization, software testing, etc. She graduated from the Saint Petersburg State University as a specialist in Mathematical Methods and Modeling in Economics. Also, she is a co-author of research papers and tutorials on efficient crowdsourcing and quality control at SIGIR, CVPR, KDD, WSDM, and SIGMOD.

🔗 https://research.yandex.com/people/603770

✉ mailto:omegorskaya@yandex-team.ru

Daria Baidakova, Yandex

Daria is responsible for consulting and educating Toloka requesters on integrating crowdsourcing methodology in AI projects. She also manages crowdsourcing courses at top data analysis schools (Yandex School of Data Analysis, Y-Data, etc) and organizes tutorials and hackathons for crowdsourcing specialists. Daria is a co-author of four hands-on tutorials on efficient crowdsourcing (at WSDM '20, CVPR '20, SIGMOD '20, WWW'21) and a co-organizer of the crowdsourcing workshop at NeurIPS'2020. Prior to her work at Yandex, she conducted several education projects for youth while working at the UAE Minister's of Youth office in 2016–2017. She graduated from the London School of Economics and Political Science with MSc in Social Policy & Development (2018), and from New York University with BA in Economics (2017).

https://www.linkedin.com/in/dashabaidakova

mailto:dbaidakova@yandex-team.ru

References

Ittai Abraham et al. 2016. How Many Workers to Ask?: Adaptive Exploration for Collecting High Quality Labels. In *Proceedings of the 39th International ACM SIGIR Conference on Research and Development in Information Retrieval*, pages 473–482.

Michael S. Bernstein et al. 2010. Soylent: A Word Processor with a Crowd Inside. In *Proceedings of the 23Nd Annual ACM Symposium on User Interface Software and Technology*, pages 313–322.

Chris Biemann. 2013. Creating a system for lexical substitutions from scratch using crowdsourcing. *Language Resources and Evaluation*, 47(1):97–122.

Jonathan Bragg et al. 2018. Sprout: Crowd-Powered Task Design for Crowdsourcing. In *Proceedings of the 31st Annual ACM Symposium on User Interface Software and Technology*, pages 165–176.

Chris Callison-Burch and Mark Dredze. 2010. Creating Speech and Language Data With Amazon's Mechanical Turk. In *Proceedings of the NAACL HLT 2010 Workshop on Creating Speech and Language Data with Amazon's Mechanical Turk*, pages 1–12.

Xi Chen et al. 2013. Pairwise Ranking Aggregation in a Crowdsourced Setting. In *Proceedings of the Sixth ACM International Conference on Web Search and Data Mining*, pages 193–202.

Justin Cheng et al. 2015. Measuring Crowdsourcing Effort with Error-Time Curves. In *Proceedings of the 33rd Annual ACM Conference on Human Factors in Computing Systems*, pages 1365–1374.

A. Philip Dawid and Allan M. Skene. 1979. Maximum Likelihood Estimation of Observer Error-Rates Using the EM Algorithm. *Journal of the Royal Statistical Society. Series C (Applied Statistics)*, 28(1):20–28.

Seyda Ertekin et al. 2012. Learning to Predict the Wisdom of Crowds. Proceedings of the Collective Intelligence 2012.

Ujwal Gadiraju et al. 2019. Crowd Anatomy Beyond the Good and Bad: Behavioral Traces for Crowd Worker Modeling and Pre-selection. *Computer Supported Cooperative Work (CSCW)*, 28(5):815–841.

Hideaki Imamura et al. 2018. Analysis of Minimax Error Rate for Crowdsourcing and Its Application to Worker Clustering Model.

Panagiotis G. Ipeirotis et al. 2014. Repeated labeling using multiple noisy labelers. *Data Mining and Knowledge Discovery*, 28(2):402–441.

Yuan Jin et al. 2017. Leveraging Side Information to Improve Label Quality Control in Crowd-Sourcing. In *Proceedings of the Fifth Conference on Human Computation and Crowdsourcing*, pages 79–88.

Jiyi Li and Fumiyo Fukumoto. 2019. A Dataset of Crowdsourced Word Sequences: Collections and Answer Aggregation for Ground Truth Creation. In *Proceedings of the First Workshop on Aggregating and Analysing Crowdsourced Annotations for NLP*, pages 24–28.

Christopher H. Lin et al. 2014. To Re(label), or Not To Re(label). In *Proceedings of the Second AAAI Conference on Human Computation and Crowdsourcing*, pages 151–158.

Greg Little et al. 2009. TurKit: Tools for Iterative Tasks on Mechanical Turk. In *Proceedings of the ACM SIGKDD Workshop on Human Computation*, pages 29–30.

Vikas C. Raykar et al. 2010. Learning From Crowds. *Journal of Machine Learning Research*, 11:1297–1322.

Paul Ruvolo et al. 2013. Exploiting Commonality and Interaction Effects in Crowdsourcing Tasks Using Latent Factor Models. In *NIPS '13 Workshop on Crowdsourcing: Theory, Algorithms and Applications*.

Aashish Sheshadri and Matthew Lease. 2013. SQUARE: A Benchmark for Research on Computing Crowd Consensus. In *Proceedings of the First AAAI Conference on Human Computation and Crowdsourcing*, pages 156–164.

Rion Snow et al. 2008. Cheap and Fast—but is It Good?: Evaluating Non-expert Annotations for Natural Language Tasks. In *Proceedings of the Conference on Empirical Methods in Natural Language Processing*, pages 254–263.

Jing Wang et al. 2013. Quality-Based Pricing for Crowdsourced Workers. NYU Working Paper No. 2451/31833.

Peter Welinder et al. 2010. The Multidimensional Wisdom of Crowds. In *Advances in Neural Information Processing Systems 21*, pages 2424–2432.

Jacob Whitehill et al. 2009. Whose Vote Should Count More: Optimal Integration of Labels from Labelers of Unknown Expertise. In *Advances in Neural Information Processing Systems 22*, pages 2035–2043.

Ming Yin et al. 2013. The Effects of Performance-Contingent Financial Incentives in Online Labor Markets. In *Proceedings of the Twenty-Seventh AAAI Conference on Artificial Intelligence*, pages 1191–1197.

Dengyong Zhou et al. 2015. Regularized Minimax Conditional Entropy for Crowdsourcing.

Association for Computational Linguistics
209 N. Eighth Street
Stroudsburg, Pennsylvania 18360

ISBN 978-1-7138-3013-9

9 781713 830139

CURRAN ASSOCIATES INC.
proceedings.com